MERCENARIES

SOLDIERS
OF FORTUNE

· PARRAGON ·

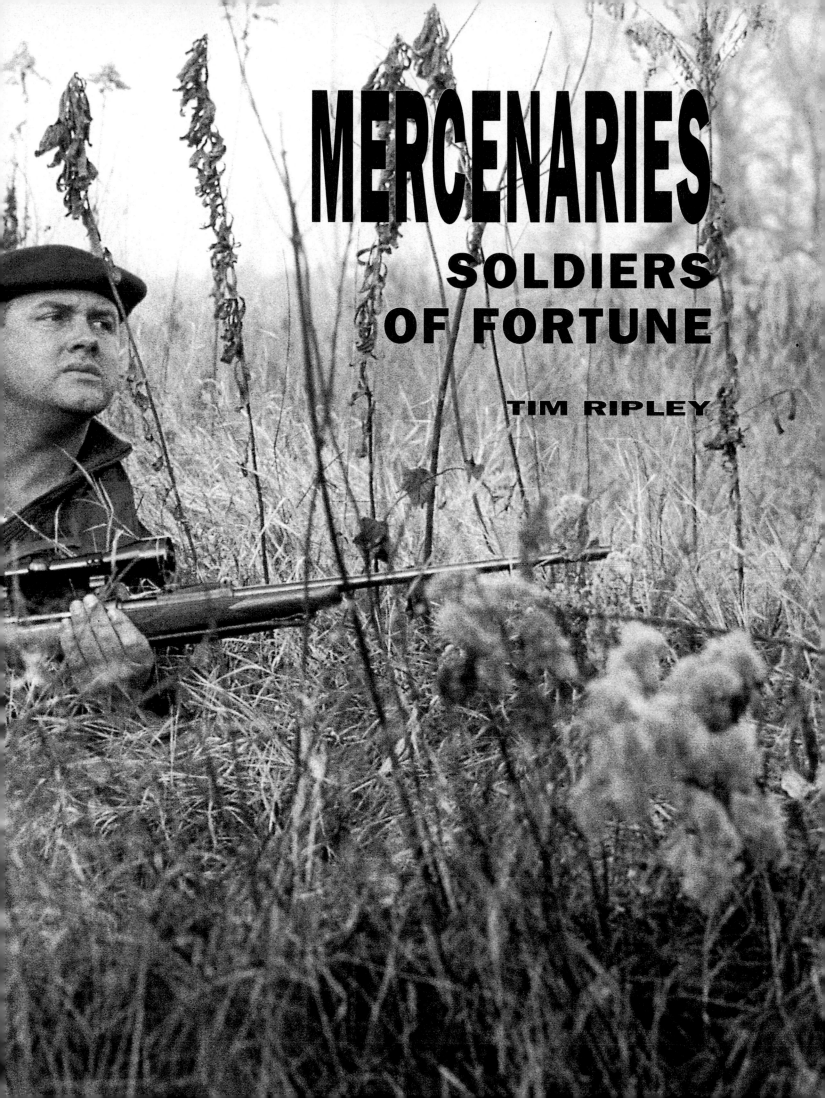

MERCENARIES
SOLDIERS OF FORTUNE

TIM RIPLEY

First published in Great Britain in 1997 by
Parragon
Units 13-17
Avonbridge Trading Estate
Atlantic Road
Avonmouth
Bristol BS11 9QD

ISBN 0-75252-232-9

Conceived, designed and produced by
Brown Packaging Books Ltd
Bradley's Close, 74-77 White Lion Street
London N1 9PF

Design: WDA

Printed in Italy

Picture Acknowledgements
Camera Press: 20, 21, 22, 23, 25 (both), 74
Photo Press: 2-3, 6, 7, 8, 14, 45, 46, 47, 50-51, 51,
52-53, 56, 57, 58, 60, 66, 68, 69, 71, 76, 77, 78,
81, 84, 85, 89, 91, 93 (bottom)
Anthony Rogers: 9, 10, 12, 13, 15 (both), 16
(both), 18 (both), 27, 28, 29, 30, 31, 32-33, 33,
34, 35, 36, 37 (both), 38 (both), 39, 40, 41, 42, 43
(both), 44, 48-49, 49 (both), 54, 72, 83, 87, 95
Frank Spooner Pictures: 58-59
TRH Pictures: 11, 17, 19, 26, 55, 61, 62, 64, 65,
73, 75, 79, 80, 82, 90, 91

Artwork Acknowledgements
Istituto Geografico De Agostini: 24, 26-27, 34-35,
52-53, 62-63, 66-67, 70-71, 86 (both), 88 (both),
92 (both), 93 (top), 94, 95 (top)

CONTENTS

CHAPTER 1

THE DOGS OF WAR

A formidable display of firepower: belts of 7.62mm ammunition used in the General Purpose Machine Gun (GPMG), a weapon popular with mercenaries, particularly former members of Britain's elite Special Air Service (SAS).

Soldiering is the world's second oldest profession, and mercenary soldiers have been lured by the promise of adventure and good money since ancient times. Today, there is still no shortage of volunteers.

'Soldiers of fortune', 'wild geese', 'contract soldiers', and 'freebooters' are some of the more colourful terms used by the popular media to describe mercenaries. When tabloid invective is flowing, they become 'hired killers' or rabid

LEFT: There are a large number of European mercenaries fighting for the Croat forces in Bosnia. The Serb forces they are opposing are resourceful, professional and better equipped.

'dogs of war'. There is an almost insatiable desire to satisfy the public's interest in so-called freelance soldiers who give up the comforts of life in the West to fight at the sharp end in other people's wars. Amid the acres of newsprint filled with mercenary stories, there is one big void. We know about their bloody exploits, but who are these people and why do they do it? Broadly speaking, a mercenary is someone who fights in a foreign army for

LEFT: A posed picture of a mercenary soldier armed with a US-made M 16. Judging by the man's headgear (an Arab khuffiah), he is on patrol somewhere in the Middle East.

World, as part of contracts to supply hi-tech weapons. Many Middle Eastern air forces can only get their aircraft into the air thanks to Western companies such as Airwork Services Ltd., British Aerospace or McDonnell Douglas, who provide ground technicians, air traffic controllers, armourers and pilots.

Secondly, there are forces involved in 'deniable operations'. When governments need to intervene discreetly in far-away countries in delicate political circumstances, and with as little fuss as possible, they will often turn to mercenaries or so-called 'private security consultants'. These operations also have the benefit of being 'deniable' if something goes wrong. In the past mercenaries have been hired by the British, French, American, Israeli and other governments to carry out covert operations and they undoubtedly will be again.

The third group are freelance contractors, classic mercenaries who will fight for anyone if the price is right, and are often involved in activities without the knowledge or approval of their government. They will work for governments, rebel groups, large multi-national companies or criminal organizations.

money, though that is a very narrow description. Mercenaries fight for different reasons, but money, idealism for a cause, and a love of action are the most common.

A simple love of adventure is a widespread reason. Inevitably, many ex-soldiers are unable to adjust to the routine of civilian life. The only job they can imagine doing is that of a soldier. This is difficult for someone without military experience to understand. Many former soldiers try to find outlets for their military talents. Some become security advisors, bodyguards or night-club bouncers. Others go one step further and take up arms in foreign war zones.

MERCENARY MOTIVES

There are four main categories of mercenary soldiers, although to a certain extent the groups are interchangeable. Firstly, official or government-sponsored troops, foreign nationals who legally enlist with a regular armed force, often with the approval and support of their own government. The Nepalese Gurkhas, who serve in the British Army, are a prime example. Governments also hire out members of their armed forces or former servicemen to other countries, particularly in the Third

THE LURE OF THE MERCENARY

Anyone who joins a combat unit in any army, in either peace or war, is indoctrinated to think that they are the best. Everyone else is regarded as a lower form of life. Combat soldiers exist only to see action. Years of training are invested in preparing them for what may only be hours, or even just minutes of war. Some soldiers will never see action at all in their military careers, but they must be ready if the call should come. After being on an adrenaline high during their time in uniform, it is impossible for some men to switch back into civilian life. Being a milkman, a factory worker or a taxi driver does not have the same appeal as military parachuting, driving a tank or flying into helicopter assaults. Nor are combat skills readily transferable to the civilian job market. Most employers prefer staff with more pacific qualifications than degrees in death and mayhem.

MERCENARIES AND INTERNATIONAL LAW

The legal status of mercenaries has always been in question. Some governments, parts of the United Nations and the media like to portray mercenaries as little better than paid killers. The show trial of the 'Angola Mercenaries' (see page 30) was the culmination of the effort to demonize the mercenary business. In most countries it is not illegal to be a mercenary, but governments can ensure that actually enlisting as a mercenary is difficult.

In Britain, under the 1870 Foreign Enlistment Act, it is illegal to recruit for foreign armies, so, for example, you can join the Foreign Legion at the French Embassy in London. The US Nationality Act supposedly prevents American citizens joining foreign armies and there are similar anti-mercenary laws in other countries. These laws have never been used in modern times and a good attorney would ensure that his client was not prosecuted should a case be brought.

The final group are volunteers, individuals who fight in foreign wars for personal or ideological reasons rather than for money. Often mistakenly termed 'mercenaries' by the press, these volunteers do not fight for personal gain. Most of the foreign volunteers who fought in former Yugoslavia were lucky to be fed by their units, let alone paid. They were there mainly to experience the thrill of battle. It is for this reason that most people attempt to join the French Foreign Legion, although the prospect of acquiring a new nationality also plays a part.

THE RULES OF WAR

Although all four categories of mercenary will be touched upon in this book, it is those in the last two categories that have attracted most media and public interest. With a popular appeal based on a mixture of adventure, espionage and war, the tabloid media are guaranteed to publicize any mercenary operation that comes to light. Although discretion is vital to their work, some mercenary leaders have a keen interest in promoting their media image as a way of acquiring additional work or attracting recruits.

RIGHT: Mercenaries are required to operate in many different environments, often at a moment's notice. Fighting in the jungle is demanding, and requires both physical and mental

Out-of-work mercenaries are also keen to make a quick buck from selling their war stories to the highest bidder.

It is often claimed that the Geneva Convention does not cover mercenaries, and this is used to justify the fact that they are sometimes executed on capture. Article 47 outlaws mercenary soldiers if they are motivated by gain and are paid more than local combatants. However, anyone who is legally recruited into an armed force, whatever their nationality, is covered by the Convention as long as they fight according to its provisions. Mercenaries often encounter problems if they are

ABOVE: A mercenary demonstrating exceptional camouflage skills, which he probably learnt as a regular soldier in one of the world's special forces units.

involved in civil wars or rebellions. Governments facing an armed rebellion rarely regard the opposition as a legitimate enemy, and treat them as rebels or war criminals. In these circumstances, mercenaries and their allies can expect little mercy if captured by government forces, and they are usually shot out of hand on the battlefield, unless, of course, their captors want to use them for propaganda purposes.

The problems that face mercenary troops are not new, as men have sold their military skills since ancient times. The Egyptians, Greeks and Romans all made extensive use of mercenary armies to police their empires, but it is in medieval Europe that we find the first mercenaries who would be recognizable to modern readers.

The alpine states of Switzerland dominated mercenary soldiering for most of the 14th, 15th and 16th centuries. Switzerland's cantons or federal regions united to fight a bloody but successful war to maintain their independence

from the Habsburg Empire in 1291. The opponents of the Habsburg emperors were keen to employ the Swiss pikemen and offered them large sums of money to fight against the Holy Roman Emperors. Initially, the impoverished Swiss cantons made official deals with prospective employers to hire out their citizen soldiers, who became the main source of government revenue. In order to maintain the state revenues stiff laws were passed to prevent freelance mercenary activities, but Swiss soldiers were in such demand that nothing could stop the flow of men to the battlefields of Europe.

THE SWISS GUARD

With the appearance of large numbers of Swiss pikemen, and later crossbowmen, on European battlefields, rulers who could not secure their services found themselves losing battle after battle. The Swiss used a closely disciplined column or phalanx that could move quickly around battlefields, seeing off charging cavalry with ease and then shattering lines of sword-wielding men-at-arms. The Swiss, being commoners from a republic without nobles, had little time for the chivalrous rules of medieval war. They only cared about winning and being paid. They gained a reputation for not taking prisoners, which was useful for intimidating enemies, but European noble rulers were aghast at the way the Swiss killed prisoners, even aristocrats.

The Swiss success in battle meant few rulers could afford not to employ them if they wanted to keep their thrones. To try to turn the tide, the Habsburgs began to create their own rival mercenary force, known as the Landsknechts, who eventually grew in size and reputation. They became great military and commercial rivals of the Swiss and gave no quarter when they met on the battlefield. Success in battle determined not only whether a soldier lived or died, but also whether he had a job, so defeat was bad for business and reduced the fees they could charge employers. The Swiss and Landsknechts developed reputations for being unscrupulous mercenaries. They knew their value, and before important battles would demand extra money or food. If their employers would not pay up, then the mercenaries sometimes left, or even changed sides.

From the 15th century until the 18th, Switzerland continued to supply most of Europe's mercenaries, hiring out its male population in their tens of thousands. The relationship between Switzerland and France was close, and the French recruited the Swiss for the prestigious Royal Guards from Louis XIV's reign until they were massacred by a mob during the French Revolution.

By 1914, freelance mercenary soldiers seemed to be superfluous The trench warfare of World War I transformed European warfare. Mass conscript armies became the dominant form of military organization as the major powers mobilized their societies for a new kind of conflict: total warfare. The heavy slaughter on the Western Front made soldiering a very unpopular profession in the decade after the Great War. It was not until the mid-1930s and the outbreak of the Spanish Civil War that large numbers of Europeans volunteered to fight in a foreign war.

THE INTERNATIONAL BRIGADES

The Spanish left-wing Republican government called for volunteers to fight off right-wing rebels led by General Franco, leading to the formation of the famous 'international brigades'. Thousands of British, French, Germans, Americans and other anti-fascist young men joined the Spanish cause. While not mercenaries in the true sense, the international brigades were to be the model for subsequent generations of young men in search of adventure, war and a 'noble' cause.

The right-wing rebels of the Spanish Civil War were supported by other types of mercenaries who would become typical after World War II. General Franco's shock troops were the Spanish Foreign Legion, which, like its French counterpart, then consisted solely of foreigners. (In 1983, Spanish nationality became a condition of enlistment.) Also supporting Franco was the German Condor Legion, which was made up of German soldiers or volunteers who covertly fought with the Spanish forces for the duration of the war.

In the decades after World War II, mercenaries would become a feature of most wars that proliferated in the wake of the Cold War, decolonization, and during the new world disorder of the 1990s, which would see mercenaries fighting on European soil once more.

FOREIGN LEGION

After the downfall of Napoleon in 1815, the restored French monarchy instantly re-established the connection with the Swiss by reforming the Swiss Guards. The French public were not impressed, however, and after the 1830 Revolution, the Swiss regiments were finally disbanded.

Less than a year later, one of Napoleon's lieutenants, Marshal Soult, recalled the Swiss to fight in the French campaign to conquer North Africa. The new Légion Étrangère was created on the condition that it would only serve outside mainland France. At first the majority of the Legion's soldiers, and all its senior officers, were Swiss. They spent almost five years in the deserts of North Africa, carving an empire that would last 130 years.

In 1835, the French hired out the Legion to the Spanish monarchy to put down a rebellion by a pretender to the Spanish throne. The Carlist Legion, which was mainly British, fought the French Foreign Legion at the Battle of Barastro in 1837 to decide the fate of Spain. Just like the Swiss and the Landsknechts 400 years earlier, the two mercenary armies fought each other with great brutality.

Just under 30 years later, the Legion spearheaded French intervention in Mexico and its greatest legend was born – Camerone. Some 60 Legionnaires were surrounded by thousands of rebels in the village of Camerone. Rejecting all calls to surrender, the last five men alive were cut down while making an incredibly brave charge at the Mexicans (illustrated above).

CHAPTER 2

THE MERCENARY BUSINESS

Individuals who come together from a variety of backgrounds to form a mercenary unit benefit from a short period of training, if only to ensure that the group bonds as a team. Here, a new recruit takes aim with an American 66mm M72 anti-tank weapon.

Mercenaries are hired by both governments and commercial organizations. Skilled and experienced soldiers can command high fees, and those with special forces' experience are highly sought-after.

Governments hire mercenaries because their official armed forces are short of men, poorly trained, badly led, under-motivated, lacking in technical expertise and under-armed. Commercial organizations turn to

LEFT: Kit from the war in Bosnia: an AK-47 lies alongside currency and photographs. The jacket sports the badge of the Croatian right-wing unit, HOS.

mercenaries when they cannot rely on the loyalty, honesty or effectiveness of the national military forces. Mercenaries are also attractive to exiled political leaders who temporarily find themselves without an army and want to regain power in their homeland. In short, mercenaries fill a gap in the military market.

Market forces dictate that clients want to use mercenaries with a proven track record. No-one wants to

GETTING TO THE WAR ZONE

International air travel makes it very easy for mercenaries to move around the world. Customs controls in Europe are all but non-existent, but in Africa, Asia and South America there are still strict border controls with visa regimes in place. Obviously, if mercenaries are on official contracts, their employers will sort out all the necessary clearances.

Freelance operations are more tricky. It does not pay to fill in 'mercenary' in the occupation section of your visa application. A good cover story is necessary, along with convincing supporting evidence, such as briefcases and suits if you are pretending to be a businessman, or sports kit for tourists. It is also unwise to walk into the airport wearing DPM combat clothing. Most personal equipment can be passed off as camping equipment, although moving weapons and ammunition is more difficult.

are immediately marketable. They have a wide range of military experience to draw upon, and have probably seen action on numerous occasions. More importantly, their military careers will have taken them to the parts of the world where their future employers live. Contacts built up during official tours of duty can soon be translated into private profit. They have the respect and trust of people in power. It is not unusual for mercenaries to be hired by their former opponents.

RECRUITMENT

Commanders with special forces experience also have good contacts with friends still in the service, who can tell them which way the political wind is blowing at home – an essential requirement if they are to operate in a politically sensitive part of the world. They can also provide tip-offs as to potential customers, or background information on employers who are bad news. Friends in high places never did anyone any harm.

Good military contacts are vital, because mercenary recruiters no longer advertise. In the 1960s and 1970s there were a couple of high profile cases of so-called mercenary recruitment agencies advertising in British newspapers. A typical ad was: 'Ex-commandos, paratroopers, Special Air Service (SAS) troopers wanted for interesting work aboard'. A deluge of prospective mercenaries responded, but many were overweight ex-soldiers with minimal job prospects at home. Most of the rest were 'wannabees' with no real military experience. In short, they were unsuitable and, more importantly, probably unreliable in a firefight. Not surprisingly, the operation ended in disaster.

Mercenary recruiters start with former military colleagues, and move on to friends of friends. This usually brings in people who have recently completed their service and are in search of the right sort of work. Many mercenary units begin to look like old-comrades' reunions. Inter-unit mixing is unusual. In Britain they tend to be either SAS-centred, Parachute Regiment-originated or Royal Marines-dominated. In France, units tend to be based on either former Foreign Legionnaires, or army paratroopers. In turn, the British tend to gravitate to the Middle East as a place to do business, and the

trust the security of their state, or even their personal protection, to soldiers who have not fired a shot in anger, will not fight when called upon, or who will turn their guns on their employers. Clients also want mercenaries who can supply a variety of skills and expertise.

It makes good sense for employers of mercenaries to sub-contract the recruitment, training, equipment and other administrative work to the leadership of the mercenary group. They are not interested in how a mercenary group is formed, just that it does its job.

Mercenary recruiters and leaders are often larger-than-life figures, almost exclusively former military men, and usually ex-officers or senior non-commissioned officers. It helps a lot if they are from elite special forces units as they

LEFT: Until recently mercenaries were recruited largely through word-of-mouth. The information super highway now provides a useful source of information and contacts.

French are more likely to work in former French colonies in Africa where their language is spoken. South Africans generally divide themselves into Afrikaans- or English-speaking units.

THE RIGHT STUFF

Recruiters prefer to employ friends and former comrades as it is easier to form an effective combat unit. Mercenary units are notoriously difficult to command because of deep personal rivalries over money, and suspicions over the motives of the unit's leadership. There is always paranoia that the operation will be betrayed, leaving members stranded alone in hostile territory far from home. Numerous operations have failed because unfamiliar mercenaries have been thrown together at short notice and expected to function as elite combat units. By sticking to old comrades, it is much easier and quicker to make the unit bond together as a team and build confidence in its mission and leaders.

The mercenary business of the 1990s is more sophisticated than in the 1960s, when mercenaries were associated with the violent and bloody civil wars in the Congo and Biafra. Then, mercenary leaders openly recruited men to serve in combat units. Such

ABOVE: *An Australian para in jungle fatigues emerges from under the wire at the Land Warfare Centre, Queensland, Australia. Paras have the 'right stuff' to be mercenaries.*

BELOW: *Regular soldiers spend years gaining skills they are unlikely ever to use in anger. For some, the opportunity to use these skills in combat only adds to the lure of mercenary work.*

opportunities are now more rare, and Western mercenaries have branched out into a wide range of activities. These range from acting as bodyguards for VIPs, providing security for valuable but vulnerable oil or mining installations, risk assessment or threat analysis of problems facing local forces, or advising on training and even public relations in war situations. Taking a mercenary force to war is now an unusual occurrence, so Western mercenaries must diversify to stay in business.

These jobs are considerably more respectable than most mercenary activity in the 1960s, and it is easy to conduct such business in Western countries. The demand for people to carry out the work is rising dramatically, so mercenary commanders have to spread their networks wider to find people of the right calibre. In Western Europe the bodyguard industry is the main source of recruits, either tapping pools of different military talent or attracting recruits straight from civilian life. The martial arts world is also regarded as a good source of both men and women who can look after themselves in a tight corner. Potential recruits are first invited to pay for the privilege of participating in a training course. No-hopers are quietly forgotten, but those with potential are given bodyguard jobs in their home country. The next step is a

job abroad. There is a very fine line between bodyguarding and being a mercenary.

Procuring the right weapons and equipment for a mercenary force is a key element in its success, so it is no surprise that there is a close link between mercenaries and the world of arms sales. The best way for mercenaries to get hold of arms is through legal channels, rather than on the black market. Illicit weapons are extremely expensive,

ABOVE: Clear, concise briefings are vital in units containing soldiers of different nationalities. A mercenary's ability to work as part of a close-knit unit is paramount, particularly as he will almost certainly be working in a country that is many thousands of miles from his own.

LEFT: Mercenary soldiers must be able to operate a wide variety of weapons from all over the world. Such technical skills are prized by governments whose troops may lack the necessary training to operate sophisticated foreign weapons.

and contact with black market arms salesmen puts the purchaser at risk of arrest.

It is surprisingly easy to buy all types of weaponry on the open (and legal) market, as long as you can pay in cash. Everything from assault rifles to light anti-tank rockets, armoured vehicles and attack helicopters is available. Governments are the best source of heavy weaponry because their activities are relatively unrestricted. Part of the mercenary contract with the client government may involve governmental supply of weapons, or the provision of valid documents, known as end-user certificates, for the purchase of weapons.

END USERS

For operations without any sort of government backing, mercenaries have to resort to black market sources for weapons. One tried-and-tested method is to secure end-user certificates from corrupt government officials. The prices vary considerably depending on the countries involved. Some African and East European governments are notoriously corrupt, and a few officials will sign anything if the price is right. With the right documents, perfectly respectable arms companies in most countries will happily release their products. Those same corrupt government officials can also be persuaded, for even larger amounts of money, to part with arms, ammunition and spare parts from official ordnance depots. They will deliver it to the user, by-passing customs and other export restrictions, such as United Nations arms export embargoes. Since the collapse of the Soviet empire in the early 1990s, Eastern Europe has become the largest growth area for the sale of black market weaponry. In return for cash, poverty-stricken soldiers and government officials have turned a blind eye to the illicit sale of billions of dollars' worth of ex-Soviet hardware. Their own governments are in dire economic straits and in many cases have not paid them a salary for years, so arms sales are the best way to feed their families. The scope ranges from a disgruntled conscript selling his AKSU assault rifle (price around $20), to a general disposing of whole depots full of artillery ($1000 per gun not including delivery).

BACK-UP

Once uniformed and equipped, a sensible mercenary is always looking to cover his back in case something goes wrong with the operation. Employers may renege on deals, or might be killed before their completion. The

ABOVE: Weapons such as this AKSU-47 have flooded onto the black market since the demise of the Warsaw Pact, sold illegally by regular soldiers trying to supplement their income.

operation could go disastrously wrong on the battlefield, or the mercenary soldiers could fall out themselves. In other words, it pays to have an escape plan ready. Cash and a valid passport are vital. It is impossible to quit Third World countries without a passport, leaving individuals at the mercy of a disgruntled and vengeful employer.

The history of mercenary soldiering is littered with cases of mercenaries being stranded in the wrong place at the wrong time because a deal has gone sour. The lucky ones have been able to use their wits to escape to safe territory; the unlucky ones either end up in jail, or worse.

One of the most common causes of the break-up of mercenary operations is disagreements about payment. Employers either abandon deals or claim the mercenaries have not completed their side of the bargain.

The famous Congo mercenaries of the 1960s had very complex contracts that covered almost every aspect of the soldiers' employment, from recruitment, pay, food, and accommodation, to leave and life insurance. These contracts were issued by the Congo Government, and supported by both the US Central Intelligence Agency (CIA) and the Belgian Government, so the mercenaries were confident that they would be honoured, particularly the payment of life insurance to relatives in case of their death.

In freelance operations, where mercenaries are working for rebel or non-governmental organisations, such confidence is usually absent. If defeated in battle, or if the

CHAPTER 3

AFRICA: THE BLOODY BATTLEFIELD

A casualty of the Congo war. The communist-backed rebels in Congo were corrupt and poorly-organised; they were also tenacious and outnumbered the government forces, so a bitter civil war dragged on for six bloody years.

Decolonization in Africa in the 1960s provided rich pickings for mercenaries. Western commercial interests were often at odds with the new regimes and mercenaries were employed to fight their battles.

In the 1960s, Africa became the centre of the world's mercenary trade. Governments, rebel groups, Western business interests and intelligence agencies all looked to freelance soldiers to protect their interests as the continent

LEFT: French mercenaries on patrol in the Congo radio back to their headquarters. At the start of the war the mercenaries were highly organised, but the situation rapidly descended into chaos.

began its bloody walk to independence. Three years after the Katanga débâcle of 1961, mercenaries were back in the Congo, thanks to their old mentor Colonel Tshombe, who in a surprise move was made prime minister after a Chinese- and Cuban-backed revolt in the east of the country. The CIA was desperate to defeat the communist-backed rebels, and persuaded Tshombe to hire a 1000-strong mercenary force to support the corrupt or militarily inefficient. Supporting Five Commando was a mercenary air force of anti-communist Cuban exiles flying surplus World War II aircraft.

FIVE COMMANDO

While the officers were generally combat veterans, the majority of the soldiers in Five Commando needed refresher training before they could be used in action. As a result, some of the early actions were far from glorious. Hoare's strict training regime soon produced results, however, and Five Commando began to cut a swathe across the rebel-held regions.

Five Commando emphasised speed and fire power to achieve success. It relied on jeeps and trucks fitted with heavy machine guns to lead its assaults, driving at break-neck speed straight into enemy-held villages, firing at anything that moved. The shock effect of these surprise attacks was usually enough to panic the rebels, who believed that jungle spirits would protect them from bullets. Five Commando achieved rehabilitation in the eyes of the international press when they spearheaded the relief of Stanleyville, where hundreds of Europeans, including nuns and missionaries, were held hostage by the rebels. Their daring attack freed the town, and soon afterwards the rebels began to retreat. It took another year to defeat them. By then, several hundred mercenaries had served in the ranks of Five Commando for six-month periods on terms and conditions which set the precedent for many future mercenary operations.

After the departure of Hoare in November 1965, the Congo mercenaries were sucked into the double-dealing world of the country's politics. Tshombe was deposed as prime minister by General Sese Seko Mobutu, who subsequently remained in power for more than 30 years. The remaining mercenary units became involved in a coup plot to overthrow Mobutu during 1967. One group, led by Frenchman Bob Denard, tried to raise the Katangans to revolt after invading by bicycle from neighbouring Angola. In eastern Congo, another group led by the Belgian 'Black Jack' Schramme seized the border town of Bukavu.

DIRTY WAR

Several dozen mercenaries in government-held territory were rounded up and summarily executed. The remainder either fled the country, or threw their lot in with Schramme who wanted to set up a pro-Tshombe

ABOVE: Armed with modern rifles, Katangan soldiers like these were trained by Western mercenaries under the leadership of 'Mad Mike' Hoare.

and incompetent Congo army. The leader of the new mercenary unit, dubbed 'Five Commando', was a South African-based Irish man, 'Mad Mike' Hoare. He was a Katanga veteran, as were many of his officers and senior NCOs. Five Commando was run very much on British lines, with ranks, organization and etiquette straight from Queen's Regulations. The personnel were mainly South African, Rhodesian, Belgian or ex-French Foreign Legion, and the unit prided itself on its good order and discipline, particularly in comparison to the chaotic Congolese troops. The mercenaries, however, were no angels and there are plenty of documented incidents of looting, as well as the murder of prisoners. Hoare's system of appointing experienced officers and NCOs to command his units meant they were never out of control

KATANGA

One country will be forever synonymous with mercenaries – the Congo (now Zaire). In 1960, Belgium, the colonial power, was faced with a fiery nationalist movement led by Patrice Lumumba. Scared by the anti-imperialist rhetoric, the Belgians decided in early 1960 to grant the country independence by June of the same year. Within months they had pulled out, handing the Congo over to its new government led by Lumumba. It only took a few days before civil war threatened to break up the country, with the mineral-rich region of Katanga declaring independence. Backed by the Belgian company, Union Minière, the Katanga leader, Moise Tshombe, hired a 200-strong mercenary force of Belgians and South Africans, the Compagnie Internationale, to defend Katanga's independence.

Congo appealed to the United Nations for protection against the rebels, and by 1961 a 20,000-strong force advanced into Katanga. It was not long before the mercenaries and the UN were openly fighting. Despite some inspired actions, the mercenaries were outgunned and outclassed. This incident established the reputation of European mercenaries as 'hate figures' among newly independent Third World countries. Mercenaries, in this instance fighting for the opponents of the new-born nation, were now definitely 'politically incorrect' in the eyes of the UN and liberal opinion in the West.

government and protect his own large estates. Mobutu refused to negotiate and launched an offensive against the mercenaries using his elite Israeli-trained paratrooper regiments and Cuban air force. The Cubans were not keen to fight their old comrades and invariably (deliberately or otherwise) missed their targets. For over two months, the mercenaries held out in Bukavu until they were overwhelmed by Mobutu's heavy American-supplied fire power and forced to flee over the border to Rwanda. Denard's Katanga revolt was more short-lived

BELOW: Mercenaries in the Congo fought alongside locally recruited Katangan forces. The soldier on the right is wearing the cap badge of the French Foreign Legion Parachute Regt.

ABOVE: Colonel Mike Hoare's British army roots are clear in his immaculate uniform. The terms and conditions Hoare established for Five Commando set the standard for future mercenary operations.

and was defeated after a few days. Once in Rwanda, the 123 remaining mercenaries were interned in a refugee camp for five months. Mobutu wanted to extradite them as war criminals but they were eventually flown on Red Cross planes back to Europe. On arrival their passports were stamped 'Not Valid for Africa'. Within a few months, however, many of them would be back in action in the dark continent. A fitting postscript to the involvement of mercenaries in the Congo conflict was the hijacking of an airliner carrying the exiled Tshombe by a CIA-backed mercenary in June 1967. The aircraft was diverted to Algeria where the godfather of the Congo mercenaries was imprisoned until his death in 1969.

BIAFRA

The next high-profile mercenary operation of the 1960s was in the rebel breakaway province of Biafra, which was fighting for its independence from Nigeria. The leader of the Biafran independence movement, the charismatic Colonel Chukwuemeka Ojukwu, was desperate to provide his poorly armed troops with weapons and training to enable them to withstand the overwhelming fire power of the Federal Nigerian Army. He looked to mercenaries to provide the help he needed.

Unlike Tshombe in the Congo, Ojukwu did not have the services of skilled mercenary leaders to select men of the right calibre and experience from the large numbers who made their way to Biafra during 1967. The first mercenaries hired were mainly Frenchmen led by a Katanga veteran, Robert Faulques. He was apparently contracted to provide 100 men, but only managed to field 53 in the end, intending to train up the Biafrans. Faulques barely had time to issue his troops with guns, however. The French preferred to adopt a more aggressive role, and at the first opportunity staged a frontal assault on a Federal unit. The result was disaster, and five mercenaries were killed by the disciplined and resolute enemy.

STEINER AND 4TH COMMANDO

All but nine of the mercenaries decided to head for home. The nine who stayed behind proved to be more efficient operators and were soon set to work organizing the Fourth Commando Division for missions behind enemy lines. A German called Rolf Steiner emerged as the commander of this supposedly elite unit, and he appointed another mercenary to command a 'battalion' of around 1000 poorly armed and equipped Biafrans. Only one man

simply being ground down by the Federal troops and their British-supplied Saladin armoured cars. The strain affected Steiner, however, and in November he suffered a breakdown, having a vehement argument with the Biafran leader that resulted in his expulsion from the country in handcuffs. By early 1969, all of the mercenaries had left Biafra. Steiner next showed up in the Sudan later that year helping rebels fight the Khartoum government. The operation ended in disaster, with Steiner being arrested in Uganda and sent back to the Sudan for the first modern mercenary 'show trial' in August 1970. His death sentence was commuted to life imprisonment and he was released three years later.

The Biafran war seemed to take the heat out of the African mercenary business for the first half of the 1970s.

BELOW: Colonel Jean Schramme, 'Black Jack' to his troops, the Belgian mercenary commander who led the coup d'état against General Mobutu in 1967.

ABOVE: Caught in a surprise attack deep in the Congolese jungle, Katangan mercenaries prepare to return fire with a jeep-mounted .50in machine gun.

in 10 had a modern assault rifle. The rest had to scavenge for weapons from dead Federal troops and find ammunition wherever they could.

Steiner seemed to think he was a World War II Waffen-SS commander, and chose the death's head as the insignia of his division. As an ex-French Foreign Legionnaire he had a soft spot for his old comrades and more Frenchmen were sent out in early 1968, only to return home a few days later after seeing little or no action. The original mercenaries remained with the division through a series of bloody defeats into the summer and autumn. They were popular with their local troops and showed great personal loyalty to Ojukwu. With no anti-tank weapons or artillery, the Biafrans were

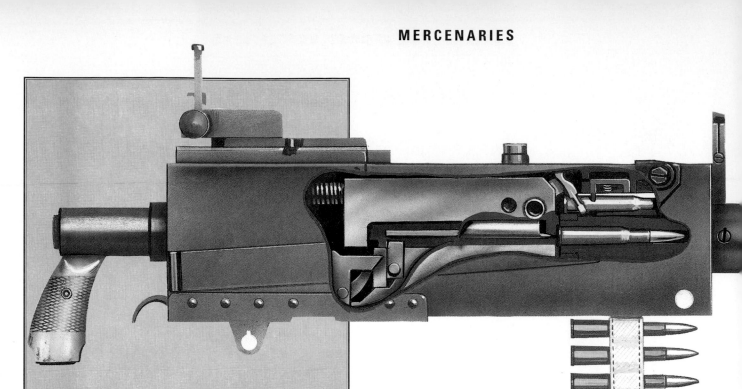

BROWNING M1919

The Browning M1919A4 medium machine gun was first used in the jeep-mounted role in World War II. One of the classic medium machine guns, the M1919 dominated firefights around the world. It remained in use for over 20 years after the end of the war, proving its worth as an effective weapon that could stand a great deal of harsh treatment. A belt-fed, air-cooled weapon, it was notable for its accuracy, reliability and ease of maintenance. Mounted on the jeeps of Five Commando, it was used to great effect in the bitter civil war in the Congo during the 1960s, and was later used throughout Africa.

Type: Browning M1919A4
medium machine gun
Calibre: 0.3in
Weight: 14.06kg (31lb)
Length: 1.044m (3ft 5in)
Effective range: 1510m (4953ft)
Rate of fire: 400-500 rounds
per minute (cyclic)
Feed: belt
Muzzle velocity: 860m
(2820ft) per second

The continent was largely at peace until the collapse of Portugal's colonial empire in Angola in 1975. With three groups fighting for power, the CIA-backed FNLA was the first to hire British mercenaries. They were recruited by the FNLA's man in England, a Bradford doctor called Donald Telford, who placed an advertisement in a newspaper to attract former paratroopers. One of this group was a dishonourably discharged British paratrooper, Costas Georgiou, who would later rise to fame under his nom de guerre, Colonel Callan.

They flew out to Zaire in late 1975 and went into Angola to join the FNLA. The scene they found was one

RIGHT: A Portuguese mercenary in a uniform similar to that worn by the South African Army, discusses the merits of grenade power with a colleague during the war in Angola in the 1970s. From a mercenary point of view, the conflict in Angola was a complete fiasco.

BELOW: *The remnants of a Soviet T54/55 MBT. The struggle for independence in Angola began in 1961 as the country's educated elite watched events in the Congo with* interest. *By 1975 there were three main groups struggling for power. British mercenaries were first employed by the FNLA, who fought the communist-backed MPLA.*

ABOVE: A rather macabre display of bloodied weapons (including an AK-47 and a rocket launcher), together with the casualty who was killed in a mercenary ambush in Angola.

of complete chaos. Just by chance, Callan was on a reconnaissance patrol and came upon a camp full of Cuban tanks and hundreds of MPLA troops. This incident was the making of Callan. He went berserk with half a dozen 66mm Light Anti-Tank Weapons (LAWs), destroying tanks and kit galore, and bringing the FNLA their first battlefield success. A grateful FNLA made Callan field commander of their army, and the CIA decided to increase the funding of its mercenary operation. South African-backed UNITA also received mercenary help from a handful of Frenchmen.

More mercenaries followed in January 1976. Some 23 were in Angola by the end of the month, but promises of modern weapons and equipment proved illusory. The mercenaries had to scavenge for uniforms and equipment in Zaire, and make up their weapons from piles of rusty scrap rifles and machine guns. They found the situation little better in Angola, but were soon involved in a series of hit-and-run raids against the MPLA. The newly arrived British mercenaries were mainly hardened professional soldiers who knew their trade and went about it with gusto. Callan may have been brave in battle, but he was hopeless as an administrator.

Callan was also paranoid about MPLA spies, and randomly shot anyone he suspected of being an enemy agent. He was so distrustful of the new, more professional arrivals that he shipped off most of them to a coastal town under the command of the British ex-SAS soldier Peter McAleese, where they were out of the way and unable to threaten his command. Callan was desperate for more men to turn back the Cuban advance of the MPLA, however, and he was impatient for Banks to generate many more recruits for his force. At the end of January, a batch of 90 mercenaries arrived at Callan's jungle base, but he immediately flew into a rage when he saw that they were not frontline soldiers, but mainly medics, mechanics and clerks. Many had never fired a shot in anger in their lives before.

ANGOLA, 1975

Callan then went off again into the bush on another raid. He returned to find his base almost deserted and most of his precious stores missing. There had been radio reports of Cuban tanks storming into the compound, but when

THE ANGOLAN WAR

Fighting broke out between Angola's three large rebel armies as they struggled for power in 1975. Each sought alliances and foreign backing in the hope of gaining control of the mineral-rich country. The Russians and Cubans supported the Marxist MPLA, the South Africans backed the UNITA guerrillas in the south of the country, and the American CIA bank-rolled the FNLA which operated in the north from Zaire. The FNLA was the smallest and least well-equipped of the three armies, and it soon found itself on the defensive as the MPLA seized the capital Luanda and started to drive northward in their Cuban-supplied tanks.

CIA chiefs were horrified. They decided to channel money through Zairian diplomats in London to a British mercenary recruiting agency run by John Banks. The former British paratrooper had already collected a card index of names of potential mercenaries from earlier ill-founded attempts to get into the business. Spurred on by a £20,000 bonus, Banks went into overdrive to mobilize his paper army.

the self-styled colonel found out the truth he was in a murderous mood. It emerged that some of the new arrivals had panicked when a Land-Rover full of mercenaries had returned to camp at night and fired a LAW at it. A large group then commandeered trucks and headed for the safety of Zaire, spreading stories of marauding Cubans and saying that the war was over. One of Callan's loyalists stopped the escaping mercenaries at the border and they sheepishly returned to camp. A livid Callan was there to meet them and he personally shot in the head the man who owned up to firing the LAW. The rest were offered one more chance to fight. Thirteen refused to fight and Callan ordered their execution. They were stripped and taken off into the bush by a team of Callan's loyalists. At the execution site they were given the chance to run before being machine gunned in the back as they escaped. Those not killed outright were shot in the head at close quarters. Again, Callan went off into

BELOW: 'Clearing by fire': sweeping the Rhodesian bush for guerrillas. Almost 40,000 guerrilla soldiers were killed in Rhodesia between 1975 and 1980.

ABOVE: A mercenary soldier carefully lays an anti-personnel mine as part of a cross-border operation during the Rhodesian war in the 1970s.

the jungle to take on the enemy. This time his luck ran out: his small team drove headlong into a major MPLA column. In the ensuing chaos, Callan was wounded and the mercenaries scattered into the bush. For days Callan hid out in a local village before being captured by patrolling MPLA troops.

Back at the Maquela base camp, the FNLA had appointed McAleese commander in the place of Callan and put Callan's henchmen on trial for the slaughter of the deserters. One was found guilty and he was shot as he attempted to escape his firing squad. Orders were issued for Callan to be shot on sight.

By now the MPLA were at the gates of Maquela, and McAleese ordered a retreat to safety in Zaire. The men out in the bush were abandoned to their fate. The handful of remaining mercenaries stood no chance of turning back the 70 Cuban tanks heading their way. Some of the men who had gone with Callan managed to walk out of the jungle, but there was no word of the colonel. Once back in the Zairian capital Kinshasa, the mercenaries were the centre of media attention as stories of the massacre of the deserters came to light. This coincided with the arrival of a new batch of 50 mercenaries who had just flown in from the UK. Everyone was just running for cover and trying to get back home as fast as possible. The British police interviewed the returning mercenaries, but no charges were ever made against any of them. A judicial inquiry was ordered under Lord Diplock into mercenary recruitment in Britain, but its recommendation for stern action was never acted upon.

The MPLA captured 13 mercenaries and tried them as war criminals in June 1976. After a highly publicised trial in front of the world's press, the Angolans sentenced Callan and three others to death. The remaining nine were sentenced to long terms in prison. Callan reportedly died bravely, facing his firing squad without emotion. His British comrade, Andy MacKenzie, who had lost a leg in action, reportedly raised himself out of his wheelchair to meet death. American Daniel Gearheart and Briton 'Brummy' Baker both went to their deaths screaming for mercy. Eight years later, all the remaining mercenaries had been released from jail in Luanda, bitter at being abandoned by their governments.

FALLOUT FROM ANGOLA

By Peter McAleese's count, some 143 mercenaries found their way into Angola during the first two months of 1976. Some 17 were killed in action, 14 were murdered by Callan, one was executed after the Maquela massacre and four were executed by the Angolans. Only 100 returned home and seven are still unaccounted for. So ended the biggest disaster in the history of British mercenary soldiering.

Mercenaries have led a number of political coups in Africa, though with varying degrees of success. In 1974, novelist Frederick Forsyth published *The Dogs of War,* which portrayed a fictional account of a mercenary unit mounting a coup d'état to seize power in a poverty-stricken West African country. Forsyth had been a reporter in Biafra, and mixed widely in mercenary circles during the late 1960s. The book described in intricate detail how the fictional coup was organised and some commentators have claimed it was the plan for a real operation that was cancelled at the last minute.

DENARD, BENIN AND THE COMOROS ISLANDS

In January 1977, a similar operation was carried out in the little-known West African country of Benin, by 60 white and 30 black mercenaries led by Bob Denard, a veteran of the Congo. The mercenaries flew into the airport at Benin's capital on a sleepy Sunday morning and quickly seized the control tower from the guards. 'Force Omega', as the mercenaries dubbed themselves, moved down town to take the presidential palace and neutralize the army barracks. The key was to kill Benin's president by mortaring his residence before launching a frontal assault. Once the president was dead, the mercenaries planned to seize the radio station to proclaim his rival, and their $500,000 paymaster, as the new president.

At first all went according to plan, but the president, by a fluke of luck, was not at home and as soon as the firefight began, he raced to the radio station to rally his troops. The mercenaries found themselves heavily outnumbered, so Denard ordered a fighting withdrawal to the airport, where their DC-7 aircraft was still waiting. Good radio communications allowed Force Omega to get away almost intact. Two mercenaries were killed and only one was left behind. Six other people died in the battle and 50 were wounded.

Within a year, Denard was back in action, but this time he managed to pull it off. He recruited the former Force Omega mercenaries, paying each one a £1000 advance, and set off for the Indian Ocean island paradise of Grand Comoro in a hired trawler. Armed only with sawn-off shotguns, the mercenaries went ashore at night by rubber dinghies. They then marched on the president's palace 4.8km (three miles) inland. They overpowered four bodyguards, killing one, and one mercenary was wounded. The mercenaries then waited for their paymaster, Ahmed Abdallah, to fly in to assume power. To avoid a counter-coup, they executed the president.

Denard was appointed minister of defence in the new government, and his 50 mercenaries became the

BELOW: During the later stages of the war in Rhodesia, mercenary troops were formed into 'fire forces' and transported to the war zone by helicopter.

backbone of the new presidential guard. They all became rich men and were given positions of influence in local society by a grateful government.

By 1989 Denard was out of favour after his men murdered President Ahmed Abdallah. He and his mercenaries staged a counter-coup and seized power for two weeks before the French Government sent 3000 troops to restore order, and the mercenaries slipped out of the country. In October 1995 the Frenchmen led another coup on the island. Again, the French Government did not approve and special forces were sent to put down the coup. Denard ended up in Le Santé jail in Paris for nine months, reportedly in a cell down the corridor from the infamous terrorist Ramirez Sanchez, also known as 'Carlos the Jackal'.

With the rise to power of pro-Moscow regimes in the former Portuguese colonies of Angola and Mozambique in 1975, the military threat to the white regimes in Rhodesia and South Africa significantly increased. African nationalist guerrillas regularly breached the borders of both countries in an attempt to end white rule. The stage was set for 15 years of brutal warfare that threatened to engulf all of sub-Saharan Africa; mercenaries played a key role in these battles.

Rhodesia was the first battle ground in the so-called 'wars of liberation'. The white minority regime of Rhodesian premier Ian Smith had declared the country independent from Britain in 1965. By 1975, after 10 years of negotiating with Britain and the African nationalists, the country's 250,000 white residents were fully mobilised for civil war in order to retain power over the country's five million black majority.

RHODESIA, 1965-80

The Rhodesian Army did not adopt a policy of formally recruiting mercenary units or paying foreigners special terms and conditions. If a man arrived in the country and declared that he wanted to fight, he was simply enrolled in the army like anyone else. They went through basic training with Rhodesian-born whites, and had to prove

themselves in action. 'I was in the Paras back in Britain' did not cut much ice in Salisbury. Rhodesia attracted men who wanted to experience the thrill of combat and were not really concerned about making money. There were some politically motivated volunteers, but they were rare. Many South Africans, British and Americans signed up simply to fight.

Former Angolan mercenary, Peter McAleese, found himself in Rhodesia, along with hundreds of British ex-soldiers interested in seeing action. McAleese entitled the Rhodesian chapter in his memoirs, 'Trigger Time', which gives some idea of the scope of the fighting. The Rhodesian military was in action on a daily basis, and hundreds of guerrillas, or 'terrs' as they were known, were killed every month. Almost 40,000 members of the guerrilla forces were killed during the last five years of the war alone.

Rhodesia's white population proved much too small to sustain the war, and in 1979 Ian Smith agreed to a British-brokered peace deal. Elections were held in 1980 and won

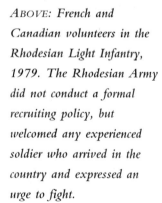

ABOVE: French and Canadian volunteers in the Rhodesian Light Infantry, 1979. The Rhodesian Army did not conduct a formal recruiting policy, but welcomed any experienced soldier who arrived in the country and expressed an urge to fight.

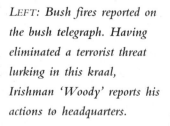

LEFT: Bush fires reported on the bush telegraph. Having eliminated a terrorist threat lurking in this kraal, Irishman 'Woody' reports his actions to headquarters.

THE RHODESIANS

During the struggle in Rhodesia in the 1960s and 1970s, foreigners who proved themselves in training were likely to find themselves in Rhodesia's elite special forces units. Generally, all-white units, such as the Rhodesia Light Infantry (RLI), Rhodesian SAS, Selous Scouts and Grey Scouts, were run on British lines.

The RLI was formed into helicopter-borne 'fire forces' that staged raids deep into neighbouring countries, or mounted search-and-destroy missions inside Rhodesia. Rhodesia's SAS followed in the tradition of its British namesake and conducted long-range patrols to locate guerrilla bases. The Selous and Grey Scouts specialised in covert reconnaissance missions and recruited former guerrillas to fight against their old comrades.

The Rhodesian Central Intelligence Organisation (CIO) and Special Branch (SB) were also keen to recruit professional military men who might be interested in what was termed 'passport work'. This involved visiting African countries under cover as European businessmen and then carrying out acts of sabotage against guerrilla bases, or assassinations of personnel hostile to Ian Smith's white-minority Rhodesian Government.

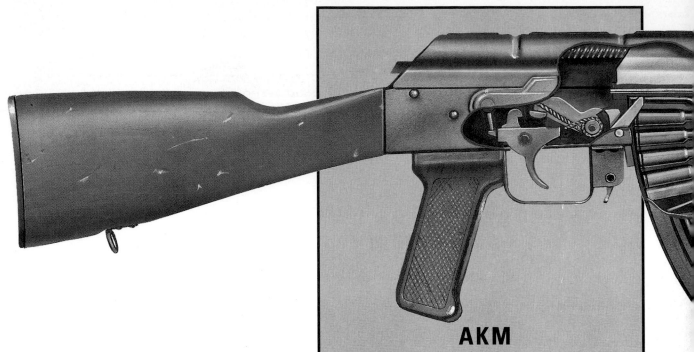

AKM

The Kalashnikov AKM is a modernized version of the AK-47. Simple, robust and reliable, it is 'soldier-proof' and differs in no fundamental feature. It is produced in two forms, as the AKM with a wooden stock, and the AKMS with a folding stock. Accurate up to 300m (984ft), it is noisy but extremely cheap and hence popular with mercenary armies. Further developments produced the AK-74, a more accurate weapon which takes 5.45mm ammunition, the Russian equivalent of the standard Nato 5.56mm round.

Type: Kalashnikov AKM assault rifle
Calibre: 7.62mm
Weight: 3.15kg (6.9lb) empty
Length: 0.876m (2ft 11in)
Effective range: 300m (984ft)
Rate of fire: 600 rounds per minute (cyclic)
Feed: 30-round box magazine
Muzzle velocity: 715m (2346ft) per second

BELOW: The unofficial shield of South Africa's Pathfinder Company, surrounded by the para wings of the unit's members. Note the rune-like design of the 44, which bears an uncanny resemblance to the insignia of the Waffen-SS – possibly not just a coincidence in apartheid South Africa.

by Robert Mugabe's Zimbabwe African National Union (ZANU) party.

SWAPO AND THE SADF

The Rhodesian special forces units slowly started to disband, and the foreigners began to drift aboard, their services no longer required in the new peaceful Zimbabwe. South Africa was the refuge for most of them, and the new war along the southwest South

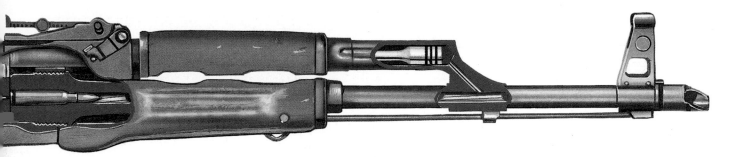

Africa/Angola border proved to be an attraction for more mercenaries in search of a 'combat high'. Pro-Moscow SWAPO guerrillas had begun a campaign to force the South Africans out of the former German colony of South-West Africa, which they had ruled since the end of World War I.

Like the Rhodesians, the South African Defence Forces (SADF) did not treat foreigners with kid gloves, and simply enrolled them in their regular units. McAleese, for example,

ended up in the Pathfinder Company of the 44 Paratroop Brigade. Others joined the special force Reconnaissance Commando or the Koevoet helicopter-borne police commando unit. Rhodesian specialists in 'turning' guerrillas found employment in 32 Battalion, which recruited former SWAPO personnel into its ranks for

BELOW: A veteran Dakota, nicknamed 'Para Dak' by the mercenaries who were paradropped over the South African-Angolan border during operations in the 1980s.

ABOVE: A rare photo of 32 Battalion operating in Angola, 1980-1. Many mercenary troops moved straight from Rhodesia to the new war in South Africa.

MERCS IN THE INDIAN OCEAN

Bob Denard's success in Grand Comoro in 1978 seemed to set off a spate of mercenary-supported coup attempts on islands in the Indian Ocean. Their small populations, combined with small and poorly armed security forces, made them plum targets. One effort involved nine British mercenaries, who were hired with promises of £10,000 each, to stage a coup on the Maldive Islands. After infiltrating the country dressed as tourists, they made a hasty retreat when the authorities were tipped off by British intelligence.

There were at least three attempts to stage a coup on the Maldives in the 10 years up to 1988. The last one took place on 3 November 1988, when more than 400 alleged Tamil mercenaries hired by a Sri Lankan poultry farmer tried to seize control of the islands in a seaborne coup attempt. Indian troops were flown in to put down the coup, and as the mercenaries escaped by boat with hostages, they were pursued and arrested by the Indian Navy.

commando raids against their old comrades. The SADF used the Rhodesian 'fire force' concept as the basis of its operations against SWAPO, but renamed its helicopter strike units 'Reaction Forces'. They reacted to daily raids along the Angolan border, and the SADF also took the offensive deep into Angola. There was plenty of 'trigger time' for all concerned, but by the end of the 1980s the South Africans had tired of the war and the heavy losses of white conscript soldiers. UN-supervised elections ended the conflict, and brought SWAPO to power in 1989. Within five years, white rule in South Africa itself would be over and many of the veteran mercenaries were out of work again.

In 1993, mercenary soldiering in Africa took a new turn when the Marxist MPLA Government in Angola turned to its former enemies to defeat the UNITA guerrilla army of Jonas Savimbi. The MPLA, recently legitimized as Angola's government by internationally

ABOVE: Following the success of the Rhodesian 'fire forces', the South Africans used helicopter 'reaction forces' to retaliate against SWAPO border raids.

sponsored elections in October 1992, hired a South African security company named Executives Outcomes (EO) to mastermind its strategy to defeat UNITA.

EO was formed by South African Afrikaans special forces veterans, and offers a complete security package to clients. These range from protecting key installations such as gold mines, through waging a small war, complete with communications, logistics, armour, attack helicopters and close air support.

Angola was EO's first big success. Former Reconnaissance Commando troopers staged raids behind UNITA lines, ex-SADF Mirage pilots took over communist MiGs and bombed rebel bases, and retired SADF brigadiers co-ordinated the war from a hi-tech communications base. By February 1995 UNITA was all but defeated. A new cease-fire was agreed and new elections took place.

SIERRA LEONE, 1995

Next on the list was war-torn Sierra Leone. In March 1995, the company was hired to defeat the rebel Revolutionary United Front who were only 30km (19 miles) from the capital Freetown. EO teams consisting of former 32 Battalion, Koevoet and the Reconnaissance Commando veterans retrained the demoralised government army and led it into action. The company also hired former SADF helicopter pilots to fly Russian-

BELOW: A French Alouette III helicopter used as a G-car (troop transport) by the South African forces in cross-border raids against SWAPO guerrillas.

ABOVE: With a heavy machine gun mounted on their vehicle, members of South Africa's Pathfinder unit patrol the Drakensberg Mountains.

BELOW: The foreign crew of an Eland armoured car are briefed prior to the 'Monte Casino' raid in September 1979. A 90mm gun is mounted on the vehicle.

made Mil Mi-17 transport helicopters. They brought in Russians to fly Mil Mi-24 gunships against the rebels in joint air–land operations that would have been familiar to Rhodesian Fire Force veterans. Some 500 EO personnel were involved in operations, and chartered aircraft delivered regular supplies from its base in South Africa.

The war was a brutal affair, with the rival forces motivated by tribal rivalries and a search for loot. Both the government and rebel soldiers could only be persuaded to go into battle if they were high on drugs. The veteran American mercenary Bob McKenzie, who was on a freelance contract in the country in 1995, was shot by the government soldiers he was supposed to be leading and left to be captured by rebels, who reportedly ate him.

EO arrived and provided advisors to the main Sierra Leone Army. The company brought in Russian APCs and trained the soldiers how to use them. EO then went on the offensive. The rebels proved hopelessly outclassed by EO's combined armour/infantry helicopter attacks and were driven back in disorder to the border. EO 'advisors' planned and led the advance, even though the company stressed its personnel were not 'combat soldiers'. The rebels were caught by surprise when EO led an armoured assault on their main base, killing 50 rebels for one EO soldier wounded. The rebels split up into some 20 small groups, and EO helicopter gunships ruthlessly chased them through the bush. Government morale soared, particularly as EO included extensive medical support in their package and made sure wounded soldiers were evacuated out of the jungle by helicopter.

By the end of 1995, the rebels had been driven back to the border regions with neighbouring Liberia, so the government could reopen its lucrative diamond mines. In return for its assistance, EO received concessions to begin mining operations itself. Similar arrangements were made with the Angolan Government. EO personnel remained in Sierra Leone throughout 1996 to ensure that the rebels were not able to regroup. A UN report accused EO of being an 'illegal mercenary operation' and 'threatening national sovereignty', and named the mining company, Branch Energy, as co-operating with EO to exploit the Koidu diamond mines in Sierra Leone. EO is also closely linked with IBIS Airline in Sierra Leone, using a Boeing 727 to fly a shuttle to South Africa. According to the UN report, EO also conducts road building, and import and export work to support its varied military operations in client countries.

BELOW: A French volunteer with the RLI strikes a pose of bravado in the Rhodesian bush. Equipped for a short-range patrol, he carries an FN FAL rifle.

THE WHITE LEGION

The refugee crisis in the Great Lakes region of Central Africa in late 1996 prompted Zairian President Mobutu to launch a major mercenary recruiting campaign. His rag-tag army had been driven out of almost all of the eastern diamond and gold rich regions of Zaire and neighbouring Rwanda by Tutsi rebels in November 1996. The international community refused to send a peacekeeping force to protect his borders from the rebels, so Mobutu turned to private enterprise to change his fortunes on the battlefield. The loss of the £1 billion Mangbwalu gold mine was a major blow to Mobutu and he was desperate to regain control of it.

French, British, South African and Angolan mercenaries were all reportedly involved, setting up a base near the rebel-held region as a springboard for Mobutu's offensive. Some 2000 foreign mercenaries gathered, supported by tanks, helicopters and fighter jets. The size and complexity of the operation suggested that Executive Outcomes was involved, but the South African company denied involvement. Paris newspapers reported that former French security officials were recruiting hundreds of mercenaries for Mobutu's so-called 'White Legion'. As of early 1997, the mercenary counteroffensive has yet to materialise, but if it does it will bring back memories of Five Commando's glory days in the Congo.

EO's client list is highly secret, but customers are believed to include Mozambique, Uganda, Zaire, Botswana, Angola, Sri Lanka and Bosnia. In spite of some harsh criticism from the South African Government and the UN, business is booming for EO. EO dismissed the UN report, stating that they are a perfectly legal company providing security services to sovereign governments. Nelson Mandela's government keeps threatening to introduce laws to restrict mercenary activity, but as of early 1997, has yet to do so. The fact that EO has helped 'black' governments retain power, rather than support 'white' regimes, may well be a factor in this delay. One thing is certain, EO's personnel will be kept busy for the foreseeable future as Africa's regimes stumble toward the next century.

The next big operational area for mercenaries may well be Nigeria, where revolution and corruption are threatening the country's military regime.

CHAPTER 4

YUGOSLAVIA: THE KILLING FIELDS

For most 'internationals' or mercenaries in former Yugoslavia, the enemy was the 'Chetnik', the Serbian soldier. Impervious to the opinion of Western Europe, this Serbian militiaman gazes impassively out of his makeshift but well-equipped bunker at Majevica, Bosnia, 1992.

Since 1992 mercenaries have been involved in the civil war in what was Yugoslavia. They have found rich pickings, as well as a brutal type of conflict that has not been seen on mainland Europe for over 50 years.

Europe's bloodiest conflict since World War II was inevitably the centre of attention for the world's professional fighting men, who travelled to the former Yugoslavia in their hundreds from 1991 looking for action

LEFT: Keith, a former Royal Marine, in a different uniform as one of 'Djuro's Men', February 1992. The war in former Yugoslavia attracted soldiers from all over the world.

and adventure. In the first two years of the war, the 'volunteers' were to the fore, but as the warring factions became organised they started to spend a large part of their black market fortunes hiring specialist military help.

After Slovenia's declaration of independence in 1991, it became clear that the nationalist government in Zagreb in neighbouring Croatia was determined to break away from Belgrade. Serbs living inside the borders of the Croat

BACKGROUND

In the summer of 1991, the country known to the world as the Socialist Federal Republic of Yugoslavia imploded into a series of bloody and brutal civil wars which produced some of Europe's newest nation states – Slovenia, Croatia, Bosnia-Herzegovina, Macedonia, Republika Serpska, and the Federal Republic of Yugoslavia (made up of Serbia and Montenegro). These new nations were born in an orgy of bloodshed as self-proclaimed nationalist politicians, power-hungry generals, local warlords, and plain old-fashioned gangsters vied for power.

From 1990, newly-elected nationalist politicians in the old Yugoslav republics began to press for freedom from the Yugoslav regime in Belgrade. In June 1991, Slovenia upped the stakes by declaring independence. The Yugoslav Federal Army (JNA) briefly tried to put down the rebellion, but were humiliated in a series of skirmishes with the highly motivated Slovenia Territorial Defence Forces (TDF). The TDF were originally formed in every Yugoslav republic as part of the country's partisan warfare concept; every citizen was armed so that any invader could be ground down in bloody guerrilla war. Somewhat ironically, the Slovenes defeated the JNA with its own weapons and tactics.

republic were far from keen to live under nationalist rule from Zagreb, which claimed as its heroes the *Ustasha* Militia. During World War II, the *Ustasha* were allied with the Nazi occupation forces and had been implicated in numerous massacres of innocent civilians. The rival propaganda of Serb and Croat politicians was a volatile brew. Within weeks, Croatia was gripped by ethnic violence, as neighbour killed neighbour. Soon the Yugoslav Federal Army (JNA) joined in, as the politicians in Belgrade showed that they could be more nationalist than their rivals in Zagreb. Bitter rivalries and hundred-year-old grudges erupted to the surface, showing that Yugoslavia had been held together by little more than the ties of communism. There is little point in trying to attribute blame; everyone had blood on their hands.

A LITTLE LOCAL DIFFICULTY

By the autumn, Croatia and Serbia were at war. There were tank battles, artillery duels, air raids, infantry assaults and plenty of massacres as well. This all made for great television coverage. The news media always need to simplify conflicts into good guys and bad guys, so it was

BELOW: A foreign volunteer fighting in the oppressive heat of a Balkan summer guards against Serbian incursions armed with a powerful 7.62mm machine gun.

Croatia's defence was chaotic, badly co-ordinated and very patchy. Local leaders emerged who took command of the units or armed men in the neighbourhood. They took orders from no-one but their own boss. The crisis staffs with military experience were able to fend off Serb attacks, but less well-prepared regions fell victim to what became known as 'ethnic cleansing'. While the Croat ministries of defence and the interior had their own units – the National Guard (ZNG), Interior Police and Special Police, and later the Croatian army (*Hrvasti Vojska* or HV) – there were not many of them, nor were they well equipped, organised or trained at first. The burden of the defence of Croatia fell on the remnants of the old Territorial Defence Force (TDF) militia, which had detachments in every part of the country. Some TDF units had hidden their equipment from the JNA in the run

BELOW: A group of foreign volunteers at a checkpoint outside Zagreb. The officer at the front is a former member of Britain's Parachute Regiment, and wears the unit's red beret.

ABOVE: A major in the Croatian HOS in Zagreb. In addition to the usual weaponry and field equipment, this officer wears a flak jacket, an item highly prized and often virtually unobtainable during the Yugoslav war.

not long before the 'brave little' Croatia was standing up to 'big bad' Serbia. This analysis probably will not stand up to historical scrutiny, but at the time there seemed to be plenty of action happening in the name of a good cause, and within a few months Croatia was the mercenary capital of the world.

Of all the myths generated by the wars in the Balkans, perhaps the most enduring is that of the so-called international brigade. The American magazine *Soldier of Fortune* declared that there was an international brigade recruiting centre in Zagreb, ready to receive with open arms any foreign volunteers ready to fight and die for Croatia. Needless to say, there was no such organization.

As Croatia's nationalists prepared for their independence bid in the spring of 1991, they set up a series of 'crisis staffs' in each region, district, town and village, which were similar to the partisan strategies of World War II. It was every man, village, town or region for itself. The crisis staffs were given carte blanche to raise militias, buy arms and prepare defences in their own areas. In reality, as there was no central control or organization,

LEFT: *Two British 'internationals' with a Croatian HOS soldier, shortly after the capture of two men who assaulted Dobroslav Paraga. Dressed in a mixture of civilian and military clothes, they are armed with Kalashnikov AK-47s.*

RIGHT: *The Bosnian war ripped apart families and turned the world upside down for the whole population. It was still comparatively uncommon to see women taking part in frontline combat, however. This female sniper, armed with the ubiquitous AK-47, is a member of the Croatian HOS, a force funded largely by generous donations from expatriate Croatians.*

up to the war; others had their arms confiscated and could barely cobble together a few old shotguns or 50-year-old museum pieces.

THE INTERNATIONALS

Into this chaotic and confused situation came the first of the foreigners who wanted to fight. They were not professional mercenaries because Croatia had no money to pay them anything but beer money and a few Deutschmarks a month. They called themselves 'volunteers' or 'internationals'. Their motivations were varied. Some were inspired by the Croatian cause, particularly those with some family connection to the country. Others were unemployed ex-soldiers who wanted a new war; there were even deserters from regular armies bored by garrison life. Undoubtedly there were scores of would-be soldiers who saw the television reports of 'mercenaries in action' and fancied themselves as instant heroes. There were also a small number of criminals and psychopaths who saw the war as a chance to kill and steal with impunity.

They usually hitchhiked or caught the train to Zagreb. Once in the capital, they either walked into the nearest Croat barracks and offered their services, or tried to get to the front to join a unit there. There was no formal recruiting system. If the local commander liked the look of them or believed their tale of military service with assorted special forces units – usually the British SAS, Paratroopers, Royal Marines, US Special Forces or French Foreign Legion – then they were in. Some volunteers just had to travel around for a few days until they found a unit that would to take them on. Others, including some hardened combat veterans, were so horrified by the scale of the violence and the chaotic nature of the Croatian defence, that they simply caught the first train home, wondering why they had been stupid enough to get themselves involved in the first place. Generally, the Croatians were keen to employ anyone who could fire a

rifle. The arrival of foreigner volunteers was seen as a sign of international, if unofficial, support for Croatian independence, so they were almost universally welcomed, at least at first. Misbehaviour by a small number of foreigners made them less popular and, by the spring of 1992, the Croats were making serious efforts to weed them out from their military units.

COMBAT JUNKIES

No-one will ever know how many 'internationals' fought for Croatia, partly because they were never grouped into single units. Some estimates say a couple of thousand during the high point of the war in 1991, but at any one time there were probably only around 200 or so in the Croatian forces. There are no official figures for foreigners killed in the war. Several dozen is probably a conservative estimate, with hundreds wounded.

Foreigners came from almost every European country, North America, Australia and even Argentina. Canada and Australia were particularly well represented because of their large expatriate Croat communities. Not only did they supply volunteers, but they made large donations to help buy arms for the homeland, in spite of the United Nations' arms embargo. The largest contingent was the British, closely followed by the French, with the majority of these being ex-regular soldiers. They ranged from 'Ed'

THE HOS

One unit that attracted a disproportionate number of foreign volunteers in Yugoslavia was HOS, or the *Hrvatske Oruzane Snage*, the military wing of the Croatian Party of Rights (*Hrvatska Stranka Prava*). This was an extreme right-wing nationalist group with its origins in the *Ustasha* militia of World War II. They were a fiercely independent group who swore loyalty to their leader Dobroslav Paraga, rather than the Croatian Government of President Franjo Tudjman or his HDZ Party.

The HOS had even been active during the period before independence, running training camps abroad for Croatian exiles. They adopted a Nazi-style black uniform, usually overalls, and black leather combat jackets. HOS insignia featured the slogan 'For My Home I am Ready'. Linked to the funds of wealthy Croatian exiles, HOS was able to arm and equip its troops extremely well in the first months of the war. By the end of 1991, Paraga claimed to have some 8000 to 10,000 men under arms, operating in company sized groups of around 100 men. In reality, though, it was probably never more than 2000 men strong. HOS units acted as 'fire brigades' whenever a crisis developed at the front. They stormed into an area, repelled Serb incursions, and then withdrew to wait for the next crisis.

ABOVE: A former member of the British regiment the Green Howards poses next to a homely bit of graffiti scrawled on the ruins of a Bosnian building.

from Bradford, whose military experience consisted of a few months in the British Territorial Army. He had simply arrived in Croatia by train and volunteered to join the first unit he could find. He spent a few months at the front helping to carry shells in an artillery unit. At the other end was 'Dave', a former British Army paratrooper and Falklands veteran. He was a professional soldier who was quickly employed as a training NCO, running basic courses for new recruits.

There was no international brigade made up exclusively of foreign volunteers, just a section here, a platoon there, or just one man who joined a Croatian unit. Often individuals got together and formed their own unit, offering their services to commanders wherever help was required. Croatian Government attempts to control the activities of the internationals were largely half-hearted until the UN-brokered cease-fire took hold in the late spring of 1992.

The internationals were particularly attracted to the right-wing unit, *Hrvatske Oruzane Snage* (HOS) as they were well equipped and constantly in action – just what the 'combat junkies' were after. Casualties were heavy, and the Serbs never took HOS soldiers prisoner. In

November 1991, the Croat Government in Zagreb began to try to establish control over the regional crisis staff and centralize command of the war. This coincided with moves by Tudjman to neutralize rival political parties, so he arrested Paraga, the leader of HOS, on trumped-up charges of planning a coup.

HOS never recovered from this move; the military units began to fragment and were slowly merged into other Croatian units. The fanatical Serb haters and many of the internationals began to drift to Bosnia-Herzegovina, where HOS units were still largely independent and war was looming in the spring of 1992.

Foreign volunteers who managed to get to the front in the autumn and winter of 1991 were engulfed in a confused and violent conflict of an intensity that Europe had not seen since World War II. Neither the Croats nor the Serbs had large numbers of well-trained and experienced soldiers. Although there was plenty of hardware floating around the battlefield of Croatia, there were tens of thousands of 'battle virgins' on both sides. The result was indiscriminate violence without apparent purpose or strategic design.

'PREVIOUS EXPERIENCE PREFERRED...'

It was a 'come as you are war'. Uniforms, equipment and weapons were in short supply at first. The internationals tended to turn up with their own uniforms and personal equipment, and sometimes they even brought their own weapons. As time went by, most volunteers wore a mix of military kit and civvies. Soldiers liked to show their former military affiliation, so old Foreign Legion, US Army and assorted British regimental badges were common on headgear and sleeves. No-one could prove a foreign volunteer's claims about their former service, and some volunteers made highly dubious claims, hoping this would speed their entrance into the Croatian forces.

The tactical scenario at the front line revolved around low-level infantry fighting. Serbs and Croats had lived

BELOW: With a pink T-shirt ruining the effect of his camouflage gear, this mercenary soldier in Bosnia carries a US Stinger anti-aircraft missile.

MERCS OUT OF CROATIA

By the end of spring 1992, the Croat-Serb war had burnt itself out. A UN-EEC-brokered cease-fire agreement led to the UN deploying a peacekeeping force to stop the war reigniting. Having survived the Serb onslaught, Croatia was now safe, and set about consolidating its armed forces ready for the almost inevitable next round to recover the Serb-held regions of Krajina and eastern Slavonia.

Many of the international volunteers started to drift home once the war was over, and the Croatian Ministry of Defence reinforced this trend by searching out and paying off any foreigners who remained. Only those who had family ties to Croatia were allowed to stay. Some of those who had served well in recognised or official units received decorations and Croatian passports, in a manner reminiscent of the French Foreign Legion's practice. Croatia was now keen to build up its own army without relying on foreigners. Some of the more outrageous antics of the internationals added to the 'wild west' image of the country, so they were encouraged to leave. Those still in search of action headed south towards Bosnia.

side-by-side for 50 years, so the Croat-Serb frontline was initially unclear, and further confused by the presence of JNA barracks in every major town. By the autumn of 1991, the so-called 'war of the barracks' was over with the JNA driven from Croatia's major cities. The conflict switched to eastern Slavonia and the mountainous region known as the Serb Krajina, that jutted out into the centre of Croatia and then hooked around the Bosnian border.

THE BUTCHER'S BILL

By the autumn, when the foreign volunteers were in Croatia in strength, the war had started to take on a positional nature, with both sides holding fixed positions and trench lines. The world looked on in horror as ground only changed hands after bloody frontal assaults which often left hundreds dead and thousands wounded. During the Serb assault on the besieged city of Vukovar in eastern Slavonia, some 1500 Croat militiamen and HOS volunteers held off 10,000 Serbs for 87 days. The city was flattened by JNA artillery, and then the defenders were gradually starved out after numerous frontal assaults failed to dislodge them.

Most internationals found themselves attached to Croat units, which were tasked to defend their home patch, and choice of unit was almost universally a matter of chance. Often a foreigner met a countryman in a Zagreb bar who invited him to join his unit, or suggested another unit looking for recruits. Volunteers of a particular nationality tended to stick together, either because of the lack of local language skills or for self-protection. A form of 'buddy-buddy' system operated if someone got in trouble or was injured; as in all wars, volunteers hoped their mates would help them out of tight corners. Life at the front was haphazard compared to that in professional Western armies. The Croats had no logistic support system, so local commanders had to beg, steal or borrow everything from arms, ammunition, food, uniforms and vehicles, to bedding and accommodation for their troops.

The war took place in an ill-defined no man's land jam-packed with mines, ruined buildings, crippled vehicles and rotting corpses. Internationals existed on the fringe of this mayhem, living in deserted houses just behind the frontline. Along with their Croatian comrades, they went daily into trenches or frontline ruins to keep the enemy at bay. The winter of 1991/92 was cold and wet, so the internationals had to survive in mud and snow. With the Serb supremacy in artillery and mortars, the Croatian frontlines were constantly shelled, so death could come at any time. The Croats took some time to learn how to construct proper overhead protection for their trench systems, but not before hundreds of their soldiers had been injured or killed by shell flying splinters.

The internationals who had previous professional combat service were extremely valuable as snipers and the leaders of fighting patrols, where their superior military skills came into their own. The most effective ways for the Croats to strike back at the Serbs were through sniping

ABOVE RIGHT: A Croatian member of the 'Special Police Anti-Terrorist' group known as 'Djuro's Men' receives instruction from a British former soldier of the Scots Guards.

LEFT: A 19-year-old Briton from Truro mans the Croatian frontline near Karlovac in December 1991. Armed with an AK-47, he wears a mixture of camouflage patterns.

RIGHT: Cliff (wearing the beret), sits on a tank with local colleagues, Nustar, 1991. Like many of the volunteers, Cliff had a rather murky background and claimed to be AWOL from the British Army.

ABOVE: A couple of idealists admire the sign on their new bunker. Whatever the reasons for fighting in Croatia, men like these brought much-needed skills to the conflict.

and raids. An international who was a skilled sniper or excelled during hand-to-hand combat would often be promoted to command by his less experienced Croatian comrades, who were desperate for efficient leadership from competent soldiers with military experience.

The chaotic nature of the Croat forces meant internationals could come and go as they pleased from the frontline. Many spent only a few days or weeks at the front before drifting back home. One former Legionnaire, a Briton called Elliott, for example, caught a bus to a town near the front, looking for a unit to join. He almost walked into a battle when wandering around, but a sentry hiding in the ruins jumped out and stopped him going within range of the Serbs. The local Croats were initially suspicious of Elliott, but released him after a couple of hours' questioning, and he ended up in a bar which served as the rest and recreation centre for troops from the nearby frontline. During a drinking session, he met a fellow Briton serving with a local unit, and the two worked out a ludicrous plan for a major raid against the Serbs. Fortunately, when Elliott woke up late the following morning his new buddy was nowhere to be seen, and the attack never materialised. Elliott made his way back to Zagreb as soon as possible, certain he would die if he stayed anywhere near the front.

FIREFIGHTS AND FIREWATER

Duty at the front was often dull, but at any time terrifying acts of violence could occur – random shelling, snipers or a hail of bullets from what is known as 'friendly fire'.

Some foreigners became involved in blood feuds with other internationals or rival Croat units. HOS fighters, for example, demanded respect at all times and turned many Croatian bars into free-fire zones.

TALKING HEADS

The international media took an avid interest in the foreign volunteers, and provided a 'home-town boy made bad' angle on the Balkan crisis. Foreign volunteers made great stories, and many reports were riddled with clichés of the well-worn 'dogs of war' school of journalism. More importantly, the foreign volunteers provided first-hand accounts of the war in English or French or German, perfectly packaged for the home market. There was no need for journalists to interview Croats with

BELOW: Two British volunteers set up a 120mm mortar in Bosnia. Although weapons were initially in short supply, by 1992 Yugoslavia was awash with military hardware.

Croat soldiers acquired their weapon-handling skills from Hollywood movies, and tended to be very nervous the nearer they got to the front, resulting in numerous firearms accidents. There seemed to be a policy of 'shoot first, ask questions later'.

The ready availability of large quantities of strong alcohol, mainly locally brewed spirits, also resulted in many troops – on both sides – being in an almost permanent alcoholic stupor, adding to the unpredictable nature of life on the Croatian frontline. During the winter of 1991-92, as the war settled down into a stalemate, boredom and drunkenness increased, and there were a number of incidents involving foreigners who killed their comrades or local civilians. Given the anarchic nature of Croatia at this time, these occurrences were not surprising. Everybody had access to firearms, and petty disagreements influenced by drink easily escalated into mini-firefights.

unpronounceable names, who rarely spoke foreign languages. Many foreign volunteers were rather camera shy because of their previous criminal records, or because they were AWOL from the regular army back home. Some were also looking ahead to future work as mercenaries and did not want to compromise their job prospects elsewhere.

Those who were willing to talk tended to use pseudonyms. A number of internationals were very keen to co-operate with the media, either to boost the Croatian

BROWNING M2

The 0.5in Browning M2 is arguably the finest machine gun ever produced and is still in widespread service. A robust heavy machine gun, it can be mounted on a vehicle or used in the ground role as a sustained-fire weapon mounted on a tripod. It possesses an excellent capability against light armour, as it fires an effective armour-piercing round as well as ball and tracer. Its versatility made it useful and popular in Bosnia.

Type: Browning M2HB heavy machine gun
Calibre: 0.5in
Weight: 38.1kg (84lb)
Length: 1.654m (5ft 5in)
Effective range: 1805m (5902ft)
Rate of fire: 450-575 rounds per minute (cyclic)
Feed: belt
Muzzle velocity: 884m (2900ft) per second

propaganda campaign, or to enhance their own macho image. They obviously loved posing for the camera, and revelled in the glory of being referred to as a mercenary and a 'dog of war'. They had proved themselves and didn't have to do any more fighting. Generally, those interviewed on television had not been involved in any serious fighting.

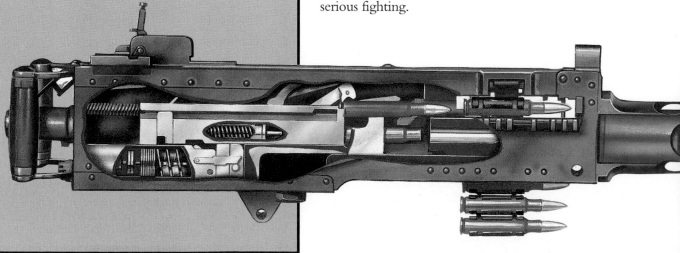

LEFT: *Two British mercenary volunteers, wearing thin snow suits over thicker layers of clothing, man a machine-gun post on the frontline in Bosnia.*

In January 1992 a freelance British journalist was shot near the frontline at Osijek, in eastern Croatia. Mystery still surrounds the incident, with the story being put out at the time that he was hit by a Serb sniper. Rumours then began to circulate that he was shot by a foreign volunteer, called 'Welshie', who was serving with the Croat forces. A British television documentary by *Observer* journalist Jon Swain followed up the story but was not able to come up with any conclusive evidence about the involvement of foreign volunteers.

With the cease-fire in Croatia, attention turned to Bosnia-Herzegovina which was a tinderbox in the spring of 1992. Croatian and Serb nationalists were angling for the right to join their brothers in Croatia and Serbia proper. The largely Muslim-led Bosnian Government in Sarajevo was moving towards declaring independence, much to the annoyance of the Serbs and Croats who would not countenance living under Muslim rule. When the Sarajevo government declared independence in April, the Serbs reacted violently and set up their own state, the

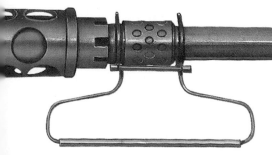

Republika Serpska. Bitter fighting broke out in Sarajevo, and all over the countryside communities took up arms to defend their homes and towns. With JNA backing, the Bosnian Serbs began to seize strategic towns and expel their Muslim or Croat populations in very brutal circumstances. Murder, torture and rape accompanied these forced population moves.

The Muslim-led army of Bosnia-Herzegovina (ABiH), like its counterpart in Croatia, was based on the old Yugoslav TDF, making every community responsible for its own defence. However, the Bosnian elements of the TDF had been largely disarmed by the JNA in the run-up to the Serb campaign, so generally the ABiH was poorly armed and equipped.

MOSTAR, 1992

In Croatian-controlled parts of Bosnia, the Croatian Defence Council (HVO) was in better shape, thanks to help from Zagreb and further afield. Many of the newly demobilized internationals in Croatia soon found themselves sent to join the ranks of the HVO and HOS units fighting in Bosnia. Their connections and experience in the Croatian armed forces meant they were

ABOVE: A Serbian militiaman armed with an M70AB2 rifle, the weapon of choice for Serb forces in Bosnia. Foreign volunteers began to move to Bosnia from Croatia in 1992.

easily assimilated into their new units. From the start, the main area of interest for the Croats was the city of Mostar, the capital of Herceg-Bosna, the self-proclaimed Croat mini-state in Bosnia. Half the city had been seized by the JNA and Serb militias, so the HVO launched a major offensive in the summer of 1992 to drive back the Serbs.

Weeks of bitter street fighting were necessary before the Serbs retreated in the face of heavy HVO and HOS pressure. Foreigners proved to be some of the HVO's best snipers during these battles. In the wake of their victory, the HVO and HOS soon disagreed, however. The extreme HOS group were too fanatical in their hatred of the Serbs for the liking of the HVO leadership, who were now more interested in 'ethnically cleansing' Mostar of its Muslim population than fighting Serbs. HOS units were recruiting as many Muslim men as possible for their offensives against the Serbs. The HVO leadership, worried that they would lose control, organized the assassination of the HOS commander in Mostar. In August, General Blaz

Krajlevic and five of his bodyguards were gunned down in an ambush outside Mostar by HVO assassins. HOS units were then slowly absorbed into the HVO, and its Muslim soldiers forced to join the ABiH.

In the northeast of Bosnia, the Croats pushed many men across the River Sava to prevent the Serbs taking over the strategically important region. HOS units containing many foreign volunteers played a major part in a desperate battle to hold the Brcko corridor that linked Serbia with the Krajina region.

THE WAR MOVES TO BOSNIA

With the war in Bosnia dominating headlines around the world, the conflict began to attract the attention of would-be soldiers of fortune. Many thought the conflict would be similar to the Croatian war and decided to set off to join the mythical 'Bosnian international brigade' to help the 'underdog' Muslims fight off the Serbs. This would be a very different war.

Foreign volunteers heading for Bosnia during the summer and autumn of 1992 first found that it was almost physically impossible to get anywhere near the action. The Serbs and Croats controlled the country's international borders and were far from helpful to would-be defenders of Bosnia. Only the most determined foreigners managed to get into Muslim-held areas. Most foreigners ended up joining the HVO and HOS around Mostar. Those entering Bosnia needed good connections with the Croats, or had to pass themselves off as journalists or aid workers to get past checkpoints. Some just walked over the mountains from Croatia.

Westerners who did make it to Bosnia received a far from friendly welcome. The country was gripped by paranoia about Serb spies, and a foreigner descending on a Bosnian village was likely to be interrogated about his motives and past activities. There was a shortage of arms, and foreigners were usually the last to receive them. Two British volunteers, Ted Skinner and Derek McBride, were murdered in central Bosnia in February 1993, possibly in an argument with Islamic *Mujahedeen* fighters. The killings highlighted the precarious nature of life as a foreign volunteer in Bosnia. If the going got rough, either through battle wounds, injury or disagreements with locals, there was no quick escape; you couldn't hitch a lift to Zagreb to catch a train home.

Bosnia was surrounded by hostile forces, and every village was on its guard for enemy foreigners. Foreign volunteers were on their own. They lived on their wits and usually operated in pairs for protection, from both the Serbs, and disgruntled Bosnians.

An ability to speak Serbo-Croat was essential to operate with ABiH units. Those former professional soldiers who

BELOW: The effects of shellfire on a block of flats in Sarajevo, a sight that was all too common in former Yugoslavia. The residents usually sheltered in cellars or evacuated the area.

did make it into Bosnia usually found themselves running training schemes for Muslim villages. Unlike Croatia, Bosnia had not prepared for war, so secret arms supplies had not been secured, nor did the country have a wealthy exile community that was prepared to channel money and arms into the country in its hour of need.

JIHAD IN CROATIA, 1993

One group of 10 British volunteers was known to have been active with the Bosnians on Mount Igman, outside Sarajevo, in the summer of 1992, but in other parts of the country only smaller groups operated with the Muslims. A handful stayed on throughout the war, but they were the exception to the rule. It is known that one man was arrested and jailed by the Bosnians outside Sarajevo during 1995, allegedly after a gunfight with his comrades and a hand-grenade attack, although the circumstances are far from clear. The outbreak of fighting between the Muslims and Croats in January 1993 gave the foreign volunteers

BELOW: The infamous 'Sniper Alley' in Sarajevo, which was constantly under siege by mercenary snipers. Locals who tried to cross this road literally risked their lives.

serving with HVO and HOS the chance to see plenty of action. British and German volunteers had fought in Mostar and Gornji Vakuf during the brutal Croat-Muslim war that lasted for a year. Many become converts to the Croat cause and married local women. They were attracted to the Croat view of the world, with its rabid anti-Muslim propaganda and ideas of ethnic purity.

Most foreigners drifting around Bosnia and Croatia in 1992 and 1993 ended up in the HVO. It was the only choice really, because Bosnia proper was sealed off. They had little understanding of the origins of the war in the former Yugoslavia, and just wanted to see some fighting. The HVO were very choosy about their recruits and closely scrutinised foreign volunteers. Those who had little military experience were usually given menial tasks, but a few foreigners were treated with great respect, usually those who had proved themselves in the Croat-Serb war and were well connected with the HVO leadership. These well-connected individuals were given dangerous or unusual jobs, such as sabotage missions behind the lines, or escorting the movement of large amounts of money. They earned substantial fees for this kind of work.

ABOVE: A local soldier is taught the finer points of firing a 66mm US-made Light Anti-tank Weapon (LAW) by a group of volunteer mercenaries in Croatia. 'Internationals' were highly valued as instructors.

It took many months for the changing nature of the war in the Balkans to filter out to the 'wannabee' mercenaries of the world. The Bosnian war was a brutal and unforgiving environment. When the murder of the two British volunteers in Travnik in 1993 received widespread publicity in Britain, it became clear that fighting in Bosnia was bad news.

While Westerners who fought in Bosnia and Croatia received a great deal of media attention, they were not the only foreigners to get involved in the conflicts in the former Yugoslavia. Serbia was supported in its war by Orthodox co-religionists from all over Eastern Europe, most of them Russians. Details about their involvement are sketchy. Although Muslim propaganda made much of stories about Cossack 'divisions' supporting the Serbs, such tales should be treated with some scepticism. More

credence should perhaps be given to reports of Romanian mercenaries fighting near Sarajevo with the Serbs in 1992. The Serbs also hired the services of the HVO during the Croat-Muslim war in 1993, with Croat helicopters and artillery assisting the Serbs in return for prompt payment in Deutschmarks. The Serbs paid back the HVO by flying in supplies to the Croatian pockets in central Bosnia.

THE MUSLIM BROTHERHOOD

On the Bosnian side, Iranian and other Middle Eastern volunteers fought from late 1992 onwards. There were never more than a couple of hundred at any one time and they fought mainly in central Bosnia around Travnik, against both the Serbs and Croats. There was no joint Muslim command, with rival Iranian, Saudi, Turkish and Malaysian-backed groups operating according to their own agendas. Although the *Mujahedeen* spread great fear in the Serb ranks, it seems they seldom went into action, preferring to act as trainers for ABiH units, praying, or engaging in black market activity. The Serbs became very worried about the *Mujahedeen* and panicked whenever they heard reports about their presence. The *Mujahedeen* always tried to keep away from UN and Nato peacekeeping troops in case the truth about Muslim breaches of the UN arms embargo emerged and undermined the Sarajevo Government's 'brave little Bosnia' propaganda. In late 1995, a British UN soldier killed a Muslim soldier at a checkpoint near Zenica, which launched a *Mujahedeen fatwa*, or death threat, against all British soldiers in Bosnia (irrespective of which side they fought for).

With the arrival of Nato's Peace Implementation Force in Bosnia in December 1996, the Bosnians came under tremendous pressure to expel all the *Mujahedeen* fighters. French and US troops staged a raid on a *Mujahedeen* training camp near Sarajevo, which led to the arrest of Iranian agents and the seizure of a number of terrorist-style weapons, including booby-trap devices. The Bosnians were reluctant to take action against the *Mujahedeen* because of their 'heroic' part in the war, and many had also married local women after taking Bosnian citizenship. Outside central Bosnia the *Mujahedeen* were far from popular with the Muslim population, which was largely secular and Westernised.

As soon as the ink was dry on the agreement that ended the Croat-Serb war in 1992, the Zagreb Government began a major drive to build up their armed forces ready to take on the Serbs again at the first opportune moment. Thanks to generous contributions from the Croatian exile community, the country was able to spend several hundred million dollars a year on weapons from 1992. Every conceivable item of military hardware, from Mil Mi-24 helicopter gunships, MiG-21 fighters, T-72 tanks, Grad rocket launchers, SA-10 surface-to-air missile systems to Mil Mi-8 Hip assault helicopters, were all purchased in Eastern Europe. The Croats needed experts

LEFT: Desperate wars require desperate remedies. This rather crude and dangerous flamethrower has been constructed by fitting a petrol bomb to the end of this volunteer's AK-47.

RIGHT: A young Bosnian reservist gets his first taste of frontline service. Wearing immaculate combat fatigues, he is armed with a Kalashnikov AK-47.

to teach them how to use these weapons and fly their new fleet of aircraft, however. Former East German air force pilots arrived in Zagreb to instruct the Croats in heliborne assault and bombing tactics. Unmanned Israeli aerial reconnaissance vehicles or drones were also used to overfly Serb lines and photograph their positions in order to increase Croatian reconnaissance capability.

AIR BRIDGE INTO BIHAC

Zagreb was also the centre of the resupply effort for the besieged Bosnian enclave of Bihac, which was surrounded by Serb-occupied Krajina. The only feasible way to get people, arms and money into the area was by air. From 1992 onwards, daily helicopter flights were made into hastily improvised air strips in Bihac by Mi-8 and Gazelle helicopters flying out of Zagreb's Lucko airfield. East European pilots were paid $5000 per trip by the Bosnian Army's 5th Corps to fly into Bihac, so there were always plenty of volunteers ready to risk the Serb anti-aircraft defences in the Krajina region. In August 1994, a large Antonov An-26 transporter aircraft, owned by a

Ukrainian air charter company, was shot down by the Serbs and the crew killed while making the short hop into Bihac from Croatia. UN observers found many Deutschmarks around the wrecked remains of the aircraft.

Russian pilots were employed elsewhere in Bosnia to fly the ABiH's Mi-8 helicopters into besieged enclaves for cash payments. The reliability of some of these pilots was called into question in spring 1995 when a helicopter pilot flying 150,000 Deutschmarks into Gorazde disappeared with his cargo. An angry ABiH high command asked the UN to help find the missing aircraft. Needless to say, it was never discovered.

In 1994, the Croats hired the American company Military Professionals Resource Incorporated (MPRI – see Chapter Two) to revamp its military forces. This marked the transformation of the involvement of foreigners in the conflicts of the former Yugoslavia. From being the playground of freebooting adventure seekers, the Balkans became a market place for real professional mercenary soldiers who offered their services to the highest bidders.

CHAPTER 5

BODYGUARDS AND WARLORDS

The Camel Corps. Soldiers of Trucial Oman patrol the desert in the 1970s, during the years of the Dhofar Uprising. Oman's connection with Britain has remained strong. There are a large number of freelance British military advisers in the Sultan's forces.

The line that divides bodyguards and mercenaries is a thin one. Employed by governments and international businesses, bodyguards employ the same expertise and skills as experienced mercenaries.

There has long been a close association between the worlds of the mercenary and the bodyguard. Professional soldiers who find themselves out of work have always been drawn to finding new outlets for their military

LEFT: A vital tool of the bodyguard's trade: a discreet but powerful 9mm automatic pistol tucked into a hip-hugging holster hidden underneath a suit jacket.

talents, and bodyguarding is an obvious choice. It is often the first step before taking employment as a mercenary in a war zone.

Bodyguarding is an ancient art, stretching back to Greek and Roman times. Today, US Secret Service agents and Scotland Yard's Royal and Diplomatic Protection Squad officers are perhaps the best-known official practitioners. In the 1960s, a new breed of private bodyguarding operations began to emerge as Western countries withdrew from their colonial empires and terrorism became more prevalent.

Bodyguarding is a low profile job that only really comes to public attention when something goes wrong. The assassination of US President John F. Kennedy in 1963, for example, is regarded as a major failure by the US Secret Service. The life of a bodyguard is far from easy, involving intense planning and preparation to ensure that every possible avenue of attack is safe. Bodyguards have to spend long hours with their charge, remaining alert for signs of attack. If an attack does take place, the bodyguard has to be prepared to fight off the assailants, evacuate his charge to safety, and in extreme circumstances put his body in the path of a bullet.

GUARDING THE RICH AND FAMOUS

Bodyguards are hired by a wide range of people, although the usual common denominator is wealth. Corporate executives, businessmen, diplomats, politicians, religious leaders, entertainers, royalty and aristocrats all employ bodyguards to protect them from assassination, kidnapping or just to stop them being harassed by inquisitive members of the public or media. Political leaders, royal families, senior government figures and military leaders in Western countries are protected by highly trained and well-equipped bodyguards. Private

BELOW: The constantly volatile situation in the Middle East has put bodyguards in great demand. Israeli troops, shown here in Lebanon in 1982, often go on to become bodyguards.

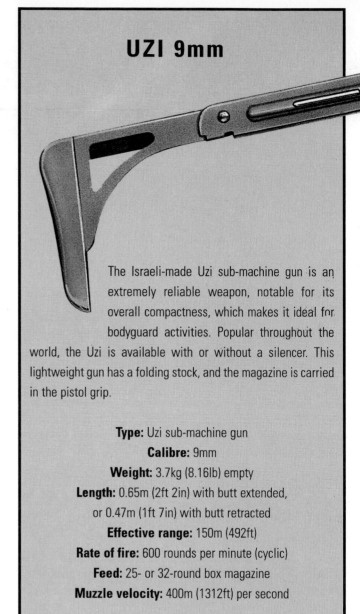

UZI 9mm

The Israeli-made Uzi sub-machine gun is an extremely reliable weapon, notable for its overall compactness, which makes it ideal for bodyguard activities. Popular throughout the world, the Uzi is available with or without a silencer. This lightweight gun has a folding stock, and the magazine is carried in the pistol grip.

Type: Uzi sub-machine gun
Calibre: 9mm
Weight: 3.7kg (8.16lb) empty
Length: 0.65m (2ft 2in) with butt extended, or 0.47m (1ft 7in) with butt retracted
Effective range: 150m (492ft)
Rate of fire: 600 rounds per minute (cyclic)
Feed: 25- or 32-round box magazine
Muzzle velocity: 400m (1312ft) per second

individuals or leaders of less developed countries have come to rely on freelance bodyguards. The most marketable people in the bodyguard world are former special forces soldiers who have received official military training in what is usually known as 'close protection' work. A bodyguard with service in a unit such as the US Delta Force, British SAS, British Royal Military Police, French Foreign Legion or Israeli *Sayeret Matkal*, will find himself in great demand.

Magazines such as *Soldier of Fortune* in America, *Combat & Survival* in the UK or *Raids* in France contain large numbers of advertisements for bodyguard courses. The applicants for these courses range from ex-soldiers in search of a way into the bodyguard and mercenary market, to 'wannabees' who have seen Hollywood movies and fancy themselves as secret agents. These courses range from basic close protection skills to full paramilitary training, encompassing hostage-rescue and escape and evasion phases. Some British companies target their courses at newly redundant soldiers, pitching their charges to match army resettlement grants.

More recently, British bodyguard companies have begun to provide National Vocational Qualifications (NVQs) for students on their courses. Students who excel on courses – which they pay for – are in the market for work with the company running the course. The others are advised to find another career.

By its very nature, bodyguarding is a far from secure job. Bodyguard companies only hire staff when they have a contract, and lay-off people when there is no work. Rates of pay also depend on the nature of the work. Home country-based jobs protecting businessmen or premises in the UK will pay considerably less than foreign missions in volatile countries.

The aim of most bodyguard firms is usually to secure steady contracts. A major source of employment for the British and French bodyguard industries has been the conflict in Algeria, which has provided a huge upsurge in long-term contracts for bodyguards and security personnel. Due to the risks involved, this is work where the rewards are high.

Links between the bodyguard and mercenary industries are close, although many on the bodyguard circuit will go to great lengths to deny any connections to the mercenary world. In many parts of the world mercenaries are associated with the 'soldiers of fortune' image, who are involved in coups d'état against legitimate governments. The bodyguard or security industry likes to be seen as providing much-needed services to legitimate governments and employers. In reality, the skills and expertise required by both types of work are very similar, and many people freely move between mercenary jobs and bodyguarding contracts. Indeed, it is very difficult to define where bodyguarding finishes and mercenary soldiering starts.

ARABIAN KNIGHTS

The Middle East is currently the best recruiting ground for mercenaries because of the region's huge oil wealth and unique system of government based on absolutist royal families. Unlike Western democracies, where citizenship implies a responsibility on every able-bodied male to serve in the armed forces in time of war, in the oil-rich emirates of the Arabian Gulf full citizenship is restricted to a small minority of the population. It is not unusual for less than

ABOVE: Evidence of the close military links between Western nations and the Middle East. A Boeing E-3 AWACS of the Royal Saudi Air, operated by freelance technicians.

20 per cent of the population to be full citizens in a Gulf state; the remainder are foreign workers who have been employed to make the country run. They do everything from emptying out rubbish bins, to administering banks, nursing in hospitals and patrolling in police cars. They have no political rights or civic responsibilities, so are not expected to fight to protect their employers in time of war. Indeed, in many places they are the subject of great suspicion. When Kuwait fell to the Iraqis in 1991, many of the foreign workers turned on their former employers. It is therefore not extraordinary that these Gulf states should employ foreigners to defend their countries and fight their wars for them. High wages and privileges ensure loyalty, and Gulf kingdoms have been hiring foreigners to fight their wars and protect their palaces for many years.

CONTRACT OFFICERS IN OMAN

The Omani Army in the 1970s, to give one example, was organized along British regimental lines, which made it easy for the contract officers to fit in. While most of the contracts were former British Army men, Australians, New Zealanders, and French Foreign Legionnaires also found their way into the Sultan's service. Their rank-and-file soldiers were mostly Baluchi tribesmen from Pakistan, a relic of the days when the Sultan's domain spread to the far side of the Indian Ocean. He retained the treaty right to recruit mercenaries from that region in much the same way as Britain is able to recruit Gurkhas from Nepal. Baluchi soldiers earned a fortune by Pakistani standards, but were only paid a fraction of what the Sultan paid his British contract officers, who earned tax-free incomes, with regular flights back to the UK. There were few native Omanis in the Sultan's army, mostly Dhofari hill tribesmen from the south, who switched sides from the rebel Dhofar Liberation Front (DLF) on the promise of cash. Indians tended to fill the administrative posts.

The British contract officers were almost all former company commanders, battalion commanders, staff officers and specialists, particularly forward observation officers trained to call in artillery fire and air support. Officers were hired on the basis of their previous military experience, and as the Sultan's British military advisers had easy access to the applicant's personal files in the British Ministry of Defence, embellishing CVs with tales of past glory was pointless. Exemplary service was rewarded with lavish gifts, promotions and large cash payments from the Sultan himself.

On operation, the contract officers lived with their soldiers in the barren mountains of Dhofar, sharing their basic rations and dangers. The British officers were recruited for their experience and tactical expertise. They led their troops for months on end in large sweeps through the Dhofar mountains to hunt down the DLF guerrillas. Contacts were brief and violent, but the superiority of the Sultan's forces in artillery and air support usually turned the tables against the DLF. Dhofar is criss-crossed by numerous mountain ridges, and moving across them, man-packing water, radios, ammunition, food, mortars and everything else a battalion needed to fight, was hard, back-breaking work. Helicopters were available for some resupply missions, but survival depended on basic soldiering skills.

The Omani Air Force was also dependent on contract personnel to keep its Skyvan transports, Strikemaster ground-attack jets and Huey transport helicopters flying. Former British Royal Air Force pilots were the Sultan's first choice, and a British company, Airwork Services Ltd., co-ordinated the logistic support of air operations.

By 1975, the war in Dhofar had largely been won, and the DLF driven back across the border into the Yemen. The Sultan did not stop hiring contract officers, however, because he needed to maintain a strong presence along the border. The SAS served with distinction in the Dhofar campaign, and a number of former SAS men have found

ESSENTIAL QUALITIES

A good military background is essential for a bodyguard. It is a job which requires proficiency in firearms, good organizational skills, leadership and fitness. More important is an ability to withstand very long periods of boredom and still be able to react to threats in split seconds. Bodyguarding in democratic Western countries is fundamentally different from operating in East European or Third World countries. In the West, bodyguards can rely on the support of efficient law enforcement agencies to help in extreme situations. Firearms are less readily available, and the local population can generally be considered friendly. Bodyguards must also abide strictly by any legal requirements covering firearms, or they could face prosecution and embarrass their charge. In other parts of the world, bodyguarding is more akin to a military operation, where no holds are barred. Participating bodyguards must be totally self-contained and cannot rely on help from the local security forces, who may be corrupt or politically hostile. For this reason, bodyguards are usually heavily armed and prepared for the worst.

BELOW: The Trucial Oman Scouts, whose uniforms bear a close resemblance to those of the British Army, were trained largely by British officers.

jobs in Oman. Even for soldiers without elite forces experience, service in the Omani armed forces continues to be a place for professional soldiers looking for a challenge and a large salary.

FREELANCE EXPERTISE

The Arabian Gulf states also employ mercenaries to protect their kingdoms. Like the Sultan of Oman, the Gulf kingdoms are keen to employ Western officers in key positions and Asians as 'foot soldiers' to do their dirty work. Bahrain's security service is still run by former British officers who are highly trusted by the ruling family. The Emir of Kuwait employs an American company to keep his M1A1 Abrams tanks in working order, and British technicians ensure his Warrior Infantry Fighting vehicles are always ready for action.

Hi-tech military equipment can now only be sold to the Middle East as part of a package that includes technicians to operate it, so Boeing had to recruit personnel to operate the Royal Saudi Air Force's E-3 AWACS radar planes. Lockheed supplied pilots to fly the Saudis' C-130 Hercules transports, Hughes Electronics operates the Saudis' air defence network, and British Aerospace pilots are at the controls of the Saudis' Tornado fighter bombers.

With the collapse of communism in Eastern Europe, the Baltic republics declared independence from Moscow

BELOW: Not the sort of belt that is traditionally worn with a business suit. This supports pistol magazines, a dagger and an electric prod, as carried by bodyguards.

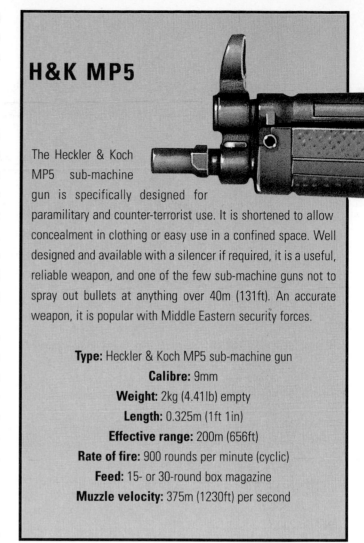

H&K MP5

The Heckler & Koch MP5 sub-machine gun is specifically designed for paramilitary and counter-terrorist use. It is shortened to allow concealment in clothing or easy use in a confined space. Well designed and available with a silencer if required, it is a useful, reliable weapon, and one of the few sub-machine guns not to spray out bullets at anything over 40m (131ft). An accurate weapon, it is popular with Middle Eastern security forces.

Type: Heckler & Koch MP5 sub-machine gun
Calibre: 9mm
Weight: 2kg (4.41lb) empty
Length: 0.325m (1ft 1in)
Effective range: 200m (656ft)
Rate of fire: 900 rounds per minute (cyclic)
Feed: 15- or 30-round box magazine
Muzzle velocity: 375m (1230ft) per second

in 1991 and were keen to establish their own security forces to provide protection from Russian attempts to re-establish Moscow's rule. Events came to a head in January 1991 when Russian special forces tried to seize key points in the Lithuanian capital Vilnius. All three Baltic states set up national police, security, counter-terrorist and defence forces. At this point, Western governments were very cautious about helping the new countries for fear of upsetting Moscow, which still claimed the right to protect Russians residing in the new states.

British, American and Scandinavian bodyguards were soon in high demand with the Baltic states, to provide training advice and protection for senior political figures in the new governments. The foreigners trained hijack rescue teams, close protection parties and made sure no harm came to the new states. The use of foreigners was important because the new governments were literally starting from scratch. They were also highly suspicious of anyone with any links to the old Soviet regime. With the

retreat of the Soviets, the Baltic states also found that they were unable to find the right calibre of people to fill the ranks of their new security and defence forces.

Increasingly, the main threat to the internal security of the Baltic states was the rise of the infamous Russian mafia, who did not shrink at murdering opponents – even government leaders – who stood in their way.

Within the new Russia, a new elite was forming to replace the old Soviet regime. Russians quickly discovered greed to replace their old belief in Karl Marx or Lenin. Russia's new capitalists found they were swimming in a sea of sharks who stopped at nothing to get their way. Many of Russia's new businesses operated on the fringes of legality, and did not care how they earned their money. This amoral business environment led to a massive rise in organized crime under the control of so-called mafia gangs or families.

The demise of the Soviet Union was also the beginning of the end of the Soviet Army. The new Russian Federation Government, along with all the other republics of the former Soviet Union, suddenly found themselves with millions of soldiers whom they could not afford to pay, feed or house. Many soldiers found themselves unpaid for months and began to look for ways to supplement their non-existent wages. Some took to selling off weapons from their barracks, others worked as taxi drivers. Many began selling their military expertise.

By the mid-1990s, Moscow was the crime capital of the world as the authorities lost control. There was a violent killing every day as mafia gangs fought for supremacy or 'eliminated' unco-operative businessmen who would not pay their 'unofficial' taxes. Drive-by shootings and grenade attacks were favourite methods of warfare. Even rocket-propelled grenades have been used to blast apart the offices of business rivals. Any businessman, banker or government official with any sense quickly hired as many bodyguards as necessary. Moscow became a battleground between rival mercenary armies of ex-Soviet soldiers. The bodyguarding business is a boom industry. Life expectancy of Russian bodyguards is measured in days or weeks, rather than years. It is dangerous work with little job security. Bodyguards are considered expendable and few tears are shed if they are killed or injured in the line of duty.

ABOVE: Former soldiers are sometimes invited to take part in bodyguard training courses. If they do well, they may be offered a job as a VIP minder.

Connections are everything in the former Soviet Union, with former members of the KGB or Spetsnaz special forces units in high demand. Some bodyguards even work on a part-time basis from their day jobs with the Russian Army. Perhaps the most famous bodyguard team in Russia are the former Soviet paratroopers who protect General Alexander Lebed. The former Russian security chief is considered a prime target for every mafia hit squad in the country because of his legendary honesty – too many people would lose money if he ever achieved his ambition of replacing Russian President Boris Yeltsin.

Mafia assassinations and organized crime have been linked to the highest echelons in the Russian Government and other former Soviet republics. Freelance military forces seem to be a useful option because they are more highly motivated and capable than their down-trodden and demoralized brethren in the official military.

UNDERCOVER OPERATIVES

America has a schizophrenic attitude to mercenaries. Ever since the War of Independence in the 18th century, when Britain used German mercenaries against the American colonists, mercenaries have been officially despised in the United States. Under the US Nationality Act, swearing allegiance to a foreign country or army can result in a US citizen being stripped of his nationality and passport.

However, since the 1950s, the US Central Intelligence Agency (CIA) has recruited large numbers of mercenaries to fight its covert wars against communist regimes in Africa, Southeast Asia and Central America. The CIA is forced to use mercenaries because of Congressional restrictions on the deployment of uniformed US servicemen in covert, undeclared wars. The use of mercenary soldiers also provides what is termed 'plausible deniability' in case anything goes wrong, so the US Government cannot be held responsible for the actions of freelance 'dogs of war' apparently acting on their own.

CUBA LIBRE

When the pro-American Cuban regime was defeated by Fidel Castro's revolution in 1959, Washington decided on covert action to remove the new government in Havana. The CIA recruited a force supposedly made up of Cuban exiles to launch an invasion of Cuba. A training base was set up in Guatemala, and recruits were flown in from Miami. They were a collection of Miami underworld low-life, fanatical anti-communist Cubans and Latin Americans in search of a quick dollar. The CIA's old China hands from CAT were called upon to form the exiles' own air force, which was now operating in the Americas under the title of Southern Air Transport. The invasion in the Bay of Pigs in April 1961 was an unmitigated disaster. The rebels found themselves out-classed by the Cubans, with some 1189 being captured and 114 killed. Two mercenary pilots, one American and one Cuban, were captured in Havana and subsequently executed, a grim example of the Cuban Revolutionaries' attitude to mercenaries. The surviving Cuban rebels went on to the Congo, where they joined 'Mad Mike' Hoare's Congo mercenaries who were also funded largely by the CIA. (See Chapter Three.)

The next CIA 'undercover' war was in Southeast Asia, where they needed to recruit a mercenary force to defend Laos from communist attack. CIA operatives 'recruited', with generous cash payments, local Hmong tribesmen and Laotian warlords to fight the communist Pathet Lao guerrillas. Supporting this secret army was the infamous Air America, another CAT off-shoot, which hired ex-USAF pilots, out-of-work airline pilots and drunks from Bangkok bars. Air America became notorious when its mercenary pilots allied with Laotian generals, who had a sideline in trading heroin, to fly their goods to market. After the official US withdrawal from Southeast Asia in

1973, the CIA turned to two Air America subsidiaries to fly supplies into the Cambodian capital Phnom Penh.

In 1976, the CIA tried to influence the civil war in Angola by supporting the FNLA and UNITA guerrillas. They recruited British and French mercenaries to fight alongside the anti-Marxist movement. Some $34 million were spent buying arms and funding mercenaries, but the open Cuba and Soviet support for the MPLA overwhelmed the CIA-backed forces.

America is the home of a unique publication: *Soldier of Fortune* magazine, published by former US Special Forces Colonel Robert K. Brown. As the self-proclaimed 'journal of professional adventurers', *SOF* magazine was first published in 1975. Brown openly declared that he would be 'going and doing' and he didn't just mean journalistically. As a Vietnam veteran who still openly espoused anti-communism, Brown was contemptuous of the Washington liberal establishment which, he believed, sold the US armed forces down the river. Along with a growing band of supporters, Brown set out to defeat communism, with or without the support of the US Government. His combat correspondents – both staffers and self-declared mercenaries – set off around the world to report from every active war zone. Usually ex-US military personnel who had turned to journalism to pay the bills, they take up arms alongside their hosts once on assignment for *SOF*. Brown has also run fund-raising events in the US to buy 'non-lethal' aid for guerrilla groups as diverse as the Nicaraguan Contras and the Afghan *Mujahedeen*.

SOLDIER OF FORTUNE

Brown and the *SOF* team appear all over the world doing their bit to turn back the 'tide of tyranny'. To date, at least five *SOF* 'correspondents' have been killed 'in action'. *SOF* could only function in America, a country where firearms legislation is such that paramilitary training is protected by the US constitution, in spite of attempts by gun control groups to limit the availability of automatic weapons. The magazine regularly publishes disclaimers, pointing out that it is illegal to recruit mercenaries in the US, but that does not stop Brown and his team 'loaning their services' to foreign armies and guerrilla groups.

Major *SOF* operations include training *Mujahedeen* guerrillas in Afghanistan, and bringing back captured Soviet weapons for the CIA. On one trip to Afghanistan,

BELOW: Defensive driving forms a vital part of a bodyguard's training. They must learn to remain calm in a crisis, while protecting their client and themselves.

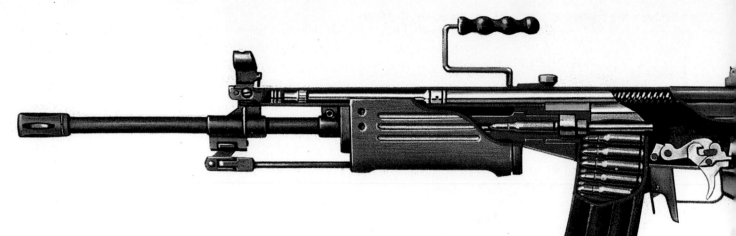

Brown was able to fulfil his ambition of personally mortaring a Red Army base. A long-term *SOF* mission was to help the Contras, at the behest of Major-General John Singlaub, who was a close associate of Colonel Oliver North. Brown and a team of ex-Vietnam vets flew into Honduras to train the Contras after the CIA pulled the plug on their support in 1984. He brought some $100,000 worth of supplies with him to make up for the loss of official US support. *SOF* personnel went regularly back and forth to the Contras throughout the 1980s, getting into some hot firefights with the Sandinistas. The El Salvador Army and its security forces were also recipients of Brown's help.

PUBLICITY STUNTS

Brown certainly knew how to generate good publicity for his magazine. He has testified before the US Senate with evidence of Soviet use of chemical weapons, and later offered a $100,000 reward to any Soviet pilot who defected with his chemical weapon spraying equipment. Brown also offered $10,000 reward to anyone who would arrest Ugandan dictator Idi Amin. He then offered $100,000 to any Nicaraguan pilot who defected with his Mil Mi-24 Hind helicopter gunship. The biggest *SOF* publicity event, however, has to be the magazine's annual convention at Las Vegas.

SOF has a particular interest in the missing in action (MIA) issue, regularly sending 'correspondents' to Southeast Asia to track down reports of US servicemen still in the hands of the communists 20 years after the end of the Vietnam War. One of his expeditions cost $250,000. Laotian tribesmen who are still fighting the

MERCS IN THE EAST

The collapse of communism in Eastern Europe has led to a spectacular growth in the recruitment of mercenaries in the former Soviet Union. The dismantling of the Soviet Union and the Warsaw Pact let loose forces of nationalism, corruption and crime that have quickly got out of control.

The withdrawal of the Soviet Army from Eastern Europe began in 1989 and quickly accelerated. By 1991, the republics on the fringes of the Soviet Union had started to stir, with the three Baltic republics – Latvia, Estonia and Lithuania – voting for independence from Moscow. In the Caucasus, independence movements also seized power and Soviet troops withdrew when it became clear that there was no stomach in Moscow for a fight to preserve its right to rule. The failed attempt by hard-line communists to seize power from reformer Mikhail Gorbachev in August 1991 signalled the end for the Soviet Union. Boris Yeltsin seized control of the Russian Federation and ordered the dissolution of the Soviet Union and the Communist Party. The Soviet Union was no more, and its constituent republics went their own ways.

These dramatic political events were accompanied by major economic upheavals as the Soviet economy fell apart, to be replaced by a primitive form of capitalism. To many, this economic system had more in common with 1920s Chicago than Western capitalism. In these circumstances crime was rampant, and law and order broke down. Political and economic power came from the barrel of a gun.

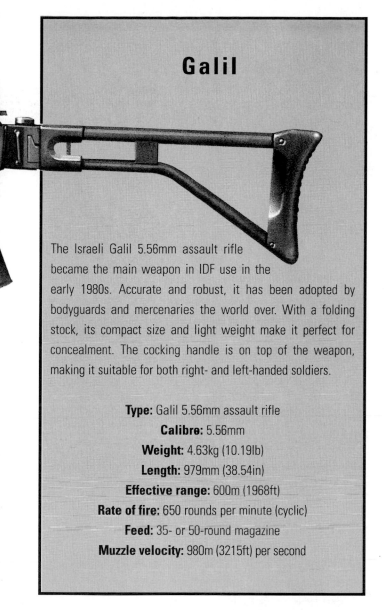

Galil

The Israeli Galil 5.56mm assault rifle became the main weapon in IDF use in the early 1980s. Accurate and robust, it has been adopted by bodyguards and mercenaries the world over. With a folding stock, its compact size and light weight make it perfect for concealment. The cocking handle is on top of the weapon, making it suitable for both right- and left-handed soldiers.

Type: Galil 5.56mm assault rifle
Calibre: 5.56mm
Weight: 4.63kg (10.19lb)
Length: 979mm (38.54in)
Effective range: 600m (1968ft)
Rate of fire: 650 rounds per minute (cyclic)
Feed: 35- or 50-round magazine
Muzzle velocity: 980m (3215ft) per second

The multi-billion-dollar drug industry, growing, harvesting and exporting illegal narcotics – primarily cocaine and heroin – to North America, appears to be a prime opportunity for mercenaries to ply their trade and make huge fortunes. The huge amounts of money generated by the drug industry mean the cartels can purchase anything they want, including the best military talent available. The lure of large sums of money can be irresistible. Edwin Wilson, a former CIA operative, who defected to Libya in 1981 as a freelance arms dealer, was not the first man to change sides for cash.

For obvious reasons, few mercenaries are willing to publicly declare their involvement with the drug cartels of Colombia or other South American countries. The most powerful drug barons are widely known to possess their own private armies to protect their drug plantations, private homes, families and export trade. In Colombia the drug cartels are, in effect, an alternative government. Their private armed forces have been known to take on and defeat Colombian Government troops and US Drug Enforcement Agency agents. The might of the US Coast Guard, as well as their formidable army of anti-narcotics agents, wages a ceaseless war against them. The drug cartels, however, are heavily armed with modern weapons. They can afford to pay high prices for experienced mercenary soldiers, who often include former members of Western special forces, compelling anti-narcotics forces to operate in large numbers and with heavy weapons support.

communists are one of Brown's soft spots because of their 'betrayal' by the CIA in 1975, so his personnel regularly travel to the Thai-Lao border region.

Brown was an early visitor to Croatia during its war against Serbia, helping to set up a number of training camps for the newly formed Croatian Army, and then the Croatian HVO in Bosnia. His 'unofficial' efforts were soon superseded by official US support for the Croats, via MPRI, and, much to his disappointment, Brown had difficulty getting to the front when the Croats launched the Krajina offensive in August 1995.

Undoubtedly the most controversial area of mercenary activity is the drug trade in Central and South America.

RIGHT: The telescopic baton, a typical concealed weapon carried by bodyguards. Its size belies how much pain it can inflict in the right hands.

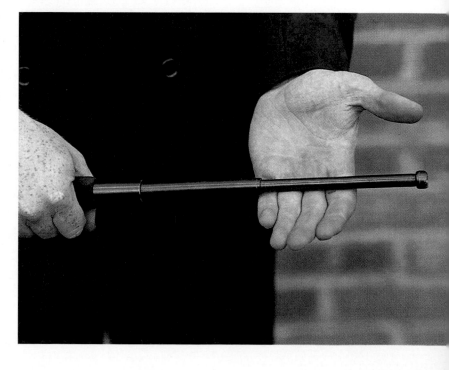

CHAPTER 6

FOREIGN LEGIONS

French Foreign Legionnaires, their Garand rifles slung over their shoulders, cross a river during France's war in Indochina in the 1950s. As in most of its campaigns, Legion soldiers paid a heavy price on behalf of politicians in Paris.

The employment of foreign legions has its roots in colonial history. The French Foreign Legion has a formidable reputation as a tough elite unit, and the Gurkhas enjoy a similar status in Britain.

Since its formation in 1831, the French Foreign Legion, or La Légion Étrangère, has been the world's most famous mercenary unit. Despite the fact that only a few hundred men every year pass the rigorous selection procedure,

LEFT: A Gurkha serving with the British Army. The Gurkhas have a fearsome reputation, and have fought for Britain with great bravery and loyalty since 1816.

thousands apply from all over the world. What is the attraction? The Legion has an awesome reputation. Its training is physically demanding, and discipline is brutal and strict. In a crisis, the Legion is always the first French unit to be dispatched, and casualties are usually heavy. With every bloody battle honour won, and despite stories about brutality during recruit training, the queues at the recruiting offices just get longer. The Legion attracts a

number of listless, bored and unemployed men who want, above all, to see combat and kill. They see the Legion as a chance to fulfil their ambitions. At the end of their service they also have the opportunity to adopt French nationality, which is a major attraction for potential recruits from East European or Third World countries. In the intervening period, they become a soldier in one of the world's fighting elites. A general in Algeria in the 1960s once declared to a new intake of recruits, 'You Legionnaires are soldiers in order to die and I am sending you where you can die.'

The Legion is not a true mercenary unit; recruits certainly do not join for money. Legionnaires are paid no more than ordinary French soldiers, and no-one ever got rich serving in the Legion. They do, however, give up any allegiance to their home countries and are expected to put loyalty to the Legion above their homeland. Indeed, at some point, they may be expected to fight their fellow countrymen.

Although the Legion still conjures up images of the desert, Beau Geste, blue greatcoats and men who need to

ABOVE: Foreign Legionnaires man a checkpoint during the invasion of Zaire (formerly Congo) in 1978, when they were sent to rescue hostages during a bloody civil insurrection.

forget their past, since World War II the Legion's history has been less exotic. However, barely a year has gone by when it has not seen action somewhere. It underwent a massive expansion to fight France's colonial wars in Indochina and Algeria. At Dien Bien Phu in 1954, the Legion's newly formed parachute battalions were surrounded and annihilated by Viet Minh guerrillas. Of the 30,000 Legionnaires who went to Indochina, almost half never returned home.

THE POST-WAR LEGION

Next, the Legion was in action against nationalist guerrillas in Algeria. This was a bloody civil war that involved all the Legion's regiments. By 1961, the French Government had given up the fight and signalled that they would grant the North African country independence. Senior French commanders in Algeria, with leaders of the expatriate community, staged a coup d'état in an attempt to overthrow President Charles de Gaulle, and used Legion paratroopers as their main shock troops. The coup was defeated and the Première Régiment Étrangère Parachutistes (1 REP) was permanently disbanded for its part in the mutiny.

In the late 1960s, the Legion was reorganized at its new bases in metropolitan France. It was to be the French army's elite rapid intervention force, designed to protect the country's interests around the world. The first major test of the new model Legion came in 1969, when 2 REP was sent to Chad in the Legion's first combat deployment since Algeria. Nine years later, the radical Libyan leader Colonel Gaddafi made the first of his attempts to gain control of the mineral-rich country. Legionnaires were sent to deter Libyan moves across the border and the situation calmed down until 1983, when open warfare broke out between French and Libyan forces. The Legion launched Operation Manta in August 1983 and brought the Libyan advance to a halt. In January 1987, the French and their allies launched a major offensive that routed the Libyans, leaving 3655 dead and 800 captured, bringing the war to an end.

The paras of 2 REP went ashore in Beirut as part of the Multi-National Peacekeeping Force in August 1982, and just over a year later some 58 French paratroopers died when an Islamic suicide bomber blew up their base in the Lebanese capital. A second force, 2 REI, was dispatched in June 1983, remaining until March 1984 and losing some half a dozen killed.

Two regiments of Legionnaires served with the French 'Daguet' Division in the Gulf War in 1991 against Iraq, where they protected the right flank of the Coalition advance into Iraq during the 100-hour ground offensive, after routing Saddam Hussein's 45th Division. The Legion was heavily committed to the United Nations Protection Force (UNPROFOR) in Bosnia, where 2 REP was the first French unit to secure Sarajevo airport at the height of the war in 1992. When the UN decided to get tough with the Serbs and dispatched the Rapid Reaction Force to Bosnia in 1995, the French Foreign Legion spearheaded the mission, occupying Mount Igman and opening convoy routes into Sarajevo. As part of Nato's Peace Implementation Force (IFOR) the Legion kept the peace in Mostar, intimidating both Croat and Muslim troops into behaving themselves.

BELOW: The Legion on parade. Never short of applicants, the Legion exercises a rigorous selection procedure, processing about 1700 recruits a year.

ORDER OF BATTLE

The French Foreign Legion now boasts some 8500 troops, of which 2000 are French officers. Almost half are based overseas to protect French interests in friendly African states and the country's remaining colonies. The elite unit is still 2 REP, which is based at Calvi in Corsica ready to respond to international crises. It has its own specialist raiding and deep reconnaissance sub-unit, the *Commandos de Renseignement et d'Action dans le Profundeur* – the famous CRAPs. The armoured infantry unit, 2ème Régiment Étrangère Infanterie (2 REI), is at Nîmes. The 1ème Régiment Étrangère Cavalerie (1 REC or the 'Spahis') at Orange has AMX-10 wheeled light tanks. Combat engineer support is provided by 6ème Régiment Étrangère Génie (6 REG) at St Morise l'Ardoise.

In Guyane (French Guiana), 3 REI guards France's remaining South American colony, and 5ème Régiment Étrangère (5 RE) stands sentry on France's South Pacific possessions, which include the notorious nuclear testing site, Murowa Atoll. Djibouti in East Africa is the home of the 13ème Demi Brigade Légion Étrangère, the Legion's oldest unit still in existence and the Legion's desert warfare specialists.

BELOW: The Legion served in the Gulf War in 1991. These troops on convoy across the desert are wearing green NBC suits and desert camo covers on their body armour.

Joining the Legion is still the stuff of legends. Today, the procedure is very routine. Prospective recruits need to get themselves to France and report to the nearest Gendarmerie Militaire (military police) or one of 23 army recruiting offices. The Gendarmerie issue would-be Legionnaires with rail warrants to the nearest recruiting office, where they undergo initial interviews and some basic selection tests. They are then dispatched to the Legion depot at Aubagne in the south of France. Here, recruits, who must be aged between 18 and 40, undergo two weeks of interviews, selection tests, security reviews (applicants with criminal records are rejected) and medical examinations. This is where recruits get their first taste of life in the Legion.

RECRUITMENT

The Legion is very selective, apparently turning away seven out of 10 applicants. Recruits still come from all over the world, with Frenchmen making up just over a third of the Legion. Britons are the next strongest contingent at 20 per cent of the strength. Germans and Americans make up to 10 per cent each. The remainder are a mix of nationalities. Eastern Europe is now a major recruiting ground.

The chosen few undergo gruelling physical tests, harried by Legion NCOs from 5 am to 10 pm. If the recruits survive the two weeks at Aubagne, they are asked to sign the standard five-year Legion contract. Five years'

honourable service makes a Legionnaire eligible for French citizenship. A pension is granted after 15 years' service, and after seven years' service a Legionnaire can marry with the permission of his commanding officer.

TRAINING

The initial instruction is rigorous, with the emphasis on physical fitness, drill, discipline and French language tuition. After 15 weeks of basic training or 'instruction' at Castelnaubary, a Legionnaire is obliged to serve until the final day of his contract with no chance of terminating or buying himself out of it as in other professional Western armies. The only way out is to desert. If deserters can escape from French territory, they are free, but will remain on the Legion's wanted list and risk arrest if they return to France. Deserting is no disgrace – only getting caught. Deserters are punished if caught; they are beaten (unofficially) and jailed. They have to complete their contract no matter how long they have been on the run.

Once instruction is complete, the Legionnaire is sent to his regiment for further specialist training – engineer, armoured, parachute, commando, radio, or logistics –

ABOVE: A British volunteer in the Legion clutches his FAMAS assault rifle prior to embarkation for the Gulf War. He wears the 'all-arms' tropical camouflage gear.

before becoming fully operational. Once with a regiment, a Legionnaire's life will revolve around his unit. They are not allowed to live outside France, and contact with families is discouraged. Legion traditions are treated with great reverence. Legionnaires can rise to be NCOs, but only long-serving soldiers can reach officer rank. Most officers are professional French Army officers who use the Legion as a fast track to promotion. Combat experience is good for their careers and they get plenty of that in the Foreign Legion.

A PASSPORT TO MERCENARY WORK

Service in the Legion has been a stepping stone in the careers of many famous modern mercenaries. Contrary to popular myth, France's legendary mercenary leader Bob Denard did not actually serve in the Legion. He was a marine infantryman, although he did fight alongside units of the Legion in Indochina and Algeria. Most of Denard's

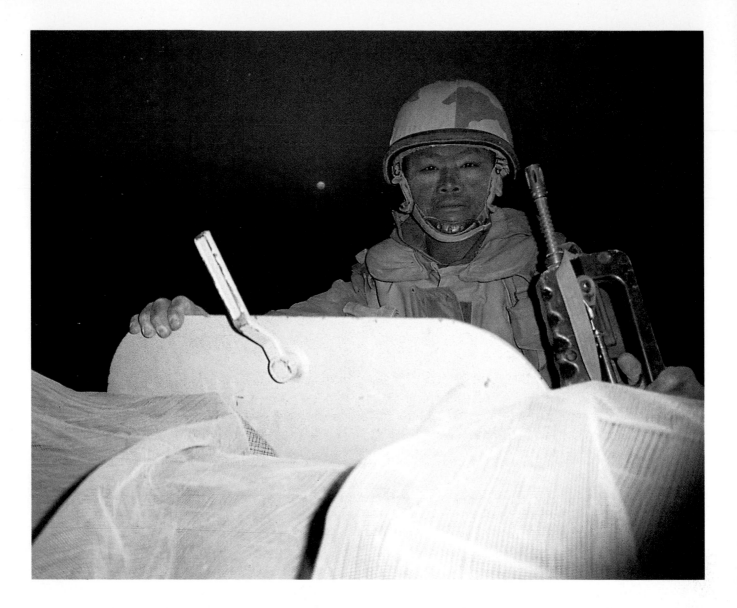

ABOVE: A Korean Legionnaire during the Gulf War. The Legion attracts recruits from all over the world. After five years' service, they are offered French citizenship.

mercenary soldiers learnt their trade in 1 REP before it was disbanded. As soon as they found themselves redundant, many quickly made their way to the Congo where they took up their old trade under new colours. As French speakers, the ex-Legionnaires were welcomed by their Belgian paymasters in the Congo. The governments of former French colonies in Africa also looked to ex-Legion soldiers to recruit and train their newly former armed forces. During his long career fighting in almost a dozen wars, Denard claimed to have commanded some 6000 men, most ex-Legionnaires; some 400 of his men have lost their lives. Veterans of 1 REP were involved in most mercenary operations of the 1960s and 1970s, but by the 1980s they were generally too old for wild adventures.

Service in the Legion continues to be a passport to other mercenary work. Recent large-scale security contracts in Algeria have drawn heavily on ex-Legionnaires who have been recruited by former senior-ranking Legion officers.

THE GURKHAS

The nearest British equivalent to a foreign legion is the Brigade of Gurkhas. Gurkha bravery is legendary. In two world wars and numerous colonial conflicts, the Nepalese hill tribesmen have covered themselves in glory in the service of the British Crown, winning 25 Victoria Crosses among many other decorations. Between 1992 and 1997, defence cutbacks slashed 5000 men from the brigade, and by early 1997, just under 3000 Gurkhas remained in British service. Thousands of Gurkhas continue to serve in the Indian Army. The Gurkhas first served the British in 1816, after the East India Company was granted the right to raise local troops in Nepal to serve in the then British-controlled Indian Army. On Indian independence in 1947, the Gurkhas were split between the British and Indians, with four of the 10 regiments remaining under British control. The symbol of Gurkhas is their famous curved kukri, a distinctive curved knife, which when used properly can be a deadly weapon. A downward blow on the head can slice a man in half. By tradition, Gurkhas are not supposed to draw their kukri without drawing blood – preferably that of an enemy.

Some 14,000 Gurkhas served with British forces in the Malay Emergency during the 1940s and 1950s, where they reinforced their reputation as fine jungle fighters, leading the battle against communist insurgents. In the 1960s, the Gurkhas were in the forefront of the Indonesian Confrontation in Borneo. It was in this conflict that Lance-Corporal Rambahadur Limbu won the most recent Gurkha Victoria Cross. The centre of Gurkha activity then moved to Hong Kong, where they secured the frontier of the British colony with communist China. In 1982, one Gurkha battalion sailed to the Falklands with the British task force to recapture the South Atlantic islands from the Argentinians. The Gurkhas' reputation alone was enough to throw the Argentine conscript soldiers into a state of terror.

The British, Indian and Nepalese governments are very sensitive to claims that Gurkha soldiers are mercenaries. They claim that the provision of Gurkha soldiers is governed by a tripartite treaty between the three governments and is more akin to the provision of assistance to allies. However, the main motivation for the Nepalese Government, and for the soldiers themselves, is financial. The British Government pays some £30 million a year in pensions to former soldiers who have retired to Nepal. Individuals selected to serve with the British Gurkhas can expect to earn almost the same as a British soldier of equivalent rank (more than £10,000 a year for a private), which is a small fortune in poverty-stricken Nepal. Those who complete their service receive a pension from the British Government, and widows of dead soldiers are also well provided for.

SELECTION AND RECRUITMENT

British Gurkhas are considered rich men to those who remain behind, so competition to secure one of the coveted places is fierce. In recent years, only one in 35 of

BELOW: Legionnaires parade in full-dress uniforms, with their famous képis and doubled 'burnous' cloaks, a legacy of the unit's North African origins.

the thousands who present themselves for the annual enlistment at the Gurkha Recruiting Depot at Pokhara are selected for British service. These numbers will be even lower in the late 1990s. The selection process is a cut-throat affair, with potential recruits vying to show the recruiting officers that they are fitter, stronger and cleverer than their rivals. They have to carry out gruelling tests of endurance, such as races up hills while carrying packs full of rocks. Successful applicants are then flown out to the Gurkha training depot for their basic training. Until recently at Se Keng, in Hong Kong, it has moved to the Gurkha Training Wing at Church Crookham in the UK in advance of the British withdrawal from the colony in June 1997. Applicants who do not make it into the British Army then put their names down for the Indian and Royal Nepalese Armies.

BELOW: Gurkhas on patrol in the jungles of Belize, 1980. Wearing standard British camouflage gear, they carry M16 rifles issued for jungle campaigns.

Under the new Brigade of Gurkhas organization, the majority of Gurkhas will serve in the United Kingdom, although most units are assigned to the new Joint Rapid Deployment Force, so can expect to be sent abroad regularly for exercises and operations. Brigade headquarters is alongside the 1st Battalion, The Royal Gurkha Rifles. This battalion is assigned to 5 Airborne Brigade in the airlanding infantry role, to follow up parachute drops by securing airfields. The Queen's Gurkha Engineers are based at Maidstone, The Queen's Gurkha Signals are located at Blandford, and The Queen's Gurkha Transport Regiment have their base at Colchester. Demonstration companies of Gurkhas are assigned to the Royal Military Academy Sandhurst and the Infantry Training Centre Brecon, to help train the British Army's officers and senior NCOs.

The 2nd Battalion, The Royal Gurkha Rifles, has remained in Brunei to help protect the oil-rich country and maintain Britain's links with the Sultan of Brunei. It remains an important location for the Gurkhas, because it is home to the British Army's jungle warfare school.

In 1996 the British Army decided to retain an extra 315 Gurkhas by forming three Gurkha reinforcement companies to boost the strength of under-recruited British battalions. The regiments receiving these soldiers were the 1st Battalion, The Royal Scots, based at Colchester as part of 24 Airmobile Brigade; the 1st Battalion, The Princess of Wales's Royal Regiment, and the 2nd Battalion, The Parachute Regiment, both of which are serving with 5 Airborne Brigade.

THE STALWART GURKHAS

Gurkha soldiers have adopted the traditions of their host units, with those serving with the Royal Scots wearing their crossed kukri badge over a Hunting Stuart tartan flash. Gurkhas serving with the Parachute Regiment have to pass the P-Company airborne selection before joining the elite airborne forces.

In spite of defence cutbacks that have cost the British army 40,000 soldiers since 1991, it continues to recruit and train Gurkhas. The attraction of Gurkhas to the British is that they are easier to recruit and train than most British soldiers. In 1996, the British infantry was some 3000 men under strength, with most battalions short of 50 to 100 men because of recruiting shortfalls; the Gurkhas, by contrast, had an unstoppable flow of recruits. Almost every Gurkhas soldier stays until the end of his contract,

unlike many British soldiers who often leave the service early. The Gurkhas represent a good return on the investment in their training. The level of fitness of Gurkhas is far superior to that of the average British recruit. Gurkha soldiers also leave their families at home in Nepal, so they have fewer welfare problems during operational deployments and they can be used more often for short-notice overseas deployments than British soldiers. Gurkhas have seen active service in Bosnia and the Gulf War, but for political reasons have yet to be deployed to Northern Ireland.

CHANGING TIMES

The Gurkha soldier of the 1990s is very different from those of earlier years who unquestioningly followed his 'sahib's' orders. Great emphasis is put on English language training, so most Gurkhas are now bilingual. The need to operate hi-tech equipment means that education standards have to be similar to those of British soldiers, with most of the tuition taking place during the recruit and trade training. Increasingly, Gurkhas are being promoted to higher ranks, and one Gurkha officer has commanded a battalion. There are now three forms of Gurkha officer: the traditional British officers are still in the majority, but they are almost equal in number to Queen's Gurkha Officers (QGO), who are commissioned former NCOs.

ABOVE: *Gurkha soldiers serving with the Sultan of Brunei's forces. Since Britain has cut back the size of her army, Gurkhas have been forced to work elsewhere.*

Commissioned Gurkha Officers (CGO) are Gurkhas with leadership potential who are sent to the Royal Military Academy, Sandhurst, to attend the same commissioning course as British officers.

The reduction in the size of the Gurkha contingent has had an unsettling affect on the brigade. This, combined with the increased exposure of the Gurkhas to Western commercial culture in Hong Kong and Europe, has led commentators to say that the Gurkhas of the 1990s are not of the same calibre as their forefathers of 30 or 40 years ago. British officers can no longer expect unquestioning loyalty and obedience. Old-fashioned 'colonial' attitudes to Gurkha soldiers will provoke adverse reactions. One company of Gurkhas were disbanded in the 1980s after their commanding officer was assaulted at a party after an exercise, and a British Gurkha officer was murdered in his office in Hong Kong by a booby-trapped grenade. The culprit was never found.

The United Nations is a supra-national organisation that has often hired freelance military expertise. Since 1990, the UN's peacekeeping and humanitarian aid operations have expanded enormously to encompass

ABOVE: A Gurkha soldier during the 1996 Nato exercise 'Purple Star'. Committed, highly skilled and brave, the Gurkhas are among the elite of the British Army.

GURKHA MERCENARIES

There are now several hundred unemployed Gurkha soldiers whose services are no longer required by the British Army. Many have returned home to join the Indian or Royal Nepal Armies. Others have gone freelance, offering their military skills to the highest bidder. Some have been hired as security guards at British embassies in unstable Third World countries. A Jersey-based company, Gurkha Security Guards Ltd., specializes in providing ex-British Army Gurkhas as bodyguards, and in early 1996 sent some 60 men to work in Sierra Leone. The British Foreign and Commonwealth Office objected to the operation because it seemed to imply official British backing for the mission. It was also a breach of the tripartite agreement which gave Britain and India sole rights to recruit Gurkha soldiers for service outside Nepal.

operations on every continent. Certain parts of the UN are ideologically opposed to the employment of mercenaries, and the Geneva Convention's famous Article 47 specifically outlaws soldiering for money. Yet other UN organizations hire ex-military personnel directly for a number of activities. UN guards in northern Iraq and a number of other aid operations are almost exclusively staffed by ex-military personnel who have been hired in to do the job. On peacekeeping operations, the UN reimburses nations who contribute their soldiers for the mission with several thousand US dollars a month, in cash. This is a lot of money for some impoverished East European and Third World countries, so they are eager to volunteer their troops to serve simply to earn hard cash. Some countries pass on a lot of this money to their soldiers, who are therefore keen to volunteer, while in many countries the money goes straight into the pockets of corrupt senior officers. This is pure mercenary soldiering in the tradition of the first Swiss mercenary brigades of the Middle Ages!

Former UN Secretary General Boutros-Boutros Ghali proposed establishing a standing UN reaction brigade to spearhead UN intervention missions. This would have been the ultimate mercenary force, but administrative and logistical complications, and the departure of the secretary general himself, have put this plan on hold

FUTURE DEMAND

It is hard to predict the future for mercenary soldiering. After the Angolan and Seychelles débâcles, mercenary soldiering seemed to go out of fashion. The famous mercenary leaders of the 1960s, such as 'Mad Mike' Hoare and Bob Denard, looked set to be figures from history, with their forces of opportunist soldiers marked as international pariahs.

As we approach the 21st century, the mercenary is back with a vengeance. Freelance military skills are back in demand. The new world order that has succeeded the Cold War confrontation between the superpowers enables any nation or military group to buy the military assistance it needs. Efforts by the United Nations to outlaw mercenaries have floundered in face of consumer demand. Even Angola's MPLA government, once in the politically correct forefront of the non-aligned world's campaign against mercenaries, has had to hire a South African mercenary company to defeat the once pro-Western UNITA guerrillas. Mercenary soldiering now encompasses a wide range of activities to meet a customer's every requirement. Staff officers, combat soldiers, technicians, fighter pilots, or any military speciality are on the market. Likewise, the arms market is wide open for anyone who needs weapons to equip his military or freelance mercenary force.

Western countries are increasingly unwilling to commit their valuable troops and limited resources to obscure conflicts in Eastern Europe, Asia or Africa, so they are more than willing to sub-contract the job to private operations, such as MPRI or Executive Outcomes. This is a formalisation of the practice established in the 1960s and 1970s, when governments used mercenaries for 'deniable' operations.

In conflicts where Western troops are likely to suffer casualties, mercenaries are always an attractive alternative. Governments will be able to send a military force to a trouble spot without worrying about casualties. The need for the services of soldiers who are willing to provide out-of-the-ordinary services will continue to grow. In the future, the West will not call upon its elite forces to intervene in crisis zones, but will hire a specialist outfit to do the job.

BELOW: The other foreign legion – soldiers of the Spanish Legion in 1982. Originally open to recruits of all nationalities, the Spanish Legion now requires recruits to be Spanish citizens.

CHAPTER 7

WEAPONS AND EQUIPMENT

The formidable Dragon anti-tank missile system, here used by an Italian soldier on a Nato exercise. Mercenaries must be familiar with many different weapons systems. The quality of their hardware depends largely on the finances of their employer.

Theoretically, mercenaries fighting in a well-organized unit should have the pick of the world's best weapons. Poorly financed operations, however, tend to acquire whatever is cheap, usually the ubiquitous Kalashnikov.

Mercenary soldiers are free from the slow bureaucratic supply chains of regular armies, so they have a reputation for arming themselves with an exotic array of weaponry. A well-financed and organized mercenary operation will

LEFT: Reliable, accurate and powerful, the Colt M16 is very popular with mercenaries. It is lightweight and superior to most European 'bullpup' rifles.

field the best weaponry money can buy. Volunteer soldiers fighting with guerrilla forces have to make do with any weapons they can get their hands on, and keep them firing with the minimum of spare parts. This chapter examines some of the most popular weapons in use with mercenaries around the world. The qualities looked for in weapons are reliability and robustness, allied to maximum stopping power.

AK-74

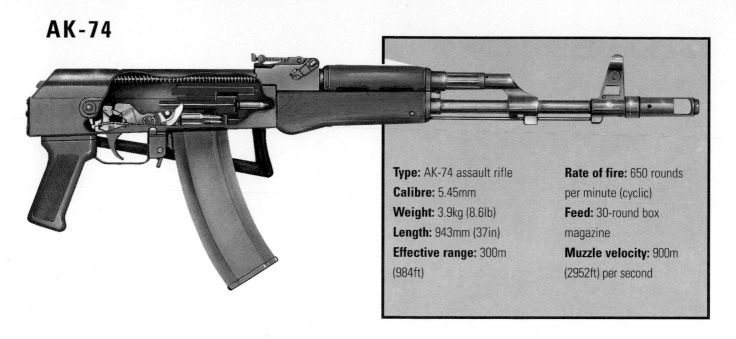

Type: AK-74 assault rifle
Calibre: 5.45mm
Weight: 3.9kg (8.6lb)
Length: 943mm (37in)
Effective range: 300m (984ft)

Rate of fire: 650 rounds per minute (cyclic)
Feed: 30-round box magazine
Muzzle velocity: 900m (2952ft) per second

ASSAULT RIFLES

AK-47/74

Since Mikhail Kalashnikov designed his classic assault rifle, the weapon has seen service in almost every conflict in the world. The AK-47, with its curved magazine, has entered popular consciousness as the symbol of Third World guerrilla fighters. Millions of copies have come off production lines in Russia, China, Romania, Yugoslavia, North Korea, Hungary, Poland, East Germany, Finland, Israel and Czechoslovakia. Given the AK's widespread availability, it is the weapon most likely to be in the hands of mercenaries and their opponents. Foreign volunteers in the former Yugoslavia were almost universally armed with AKs, and the weapon is the only one to be found in 'hot' locations in eastern Europe. In these countries it is impossible to get hold of Western 7.62mm or 5.56mm ammunition, so the AK is the only gun worth using.

Many of the AK clones feature design 'improvements', but the basic operation of the weapon is essentially similar, whatever the country of manufacture. The Russians have fielded four main versions of the weapon which have set the pace in the design of small arms.

The first AK-47 entered service with the Soviet Red Army in its basic form in 1947, chambered for 7.62 x 39mm ammunition. It had a rate of fire of 600 rounds a minute and was usually fitted with a 30-round magazine. Its range was some 1000m (3048ft). There were versions with folding and wooden stocks. A decade later, the AKM appeared, an improved version which was 25 per cent lighter and featured numerous internal changes.

The AK-74, a major re-working of the design, was manufactured in the 1970s, and was re-chambered to fire 5.45mm ammunition. It is easily recognizable by its muzzle break. During the 1980s the Soviets began to field

FN FAL

Type: FN FAL assault rifle
Calibre: 7.62mm
Weight: 5kg (11lb)
Length: 1.143m (45in)
Effective range: 500m (1640ft)

Rate of fire: 30 rounds per minute (cyclic)
Feed: 20-round box magazine
Muzzle velocity: 838m (2750ft) per second

a new mini-version of the AK, called the AKSU-74, which was intended for use with airborne, armoured and special forces troops. The weapon is only 490mm (19 in) long (730mm or 29in with folding stock extended), so it is ideal for combat in confined spaces. Since the demise of the Soviet Union, it has become the favoured weapon of Russian paramilitary policemen, bodyguards and their mafia opponents. The ability to hide it under a long coat is seen as particularly useful.

The collapse of the Soviet Empire means AKs can be bought on the black market for as little as a $30 in Russia and other east European countries. Bulk orders can result in a unit cost as low as $10 each.

FN FAL

During the 1960s and 1970s, the Belgian-designed FN FAL was the most widely available weapon of Western origin on the global arms market. Many European armies, as well as the South African and Rhodesian Armies, used it. In British Army service it was known as the L1A1 Self Loading Rifle (SLR). Most mercenaries in Africa during this period, who had previous European military service, were familiar with it as their personal weapon, and would opt for it as a matter of choice. The distinctive FN FAL, with its long, thin barrel and short, straight magazine, was easily recognizable in television coverage of the Congo, Rhodesian and Angolan conflicts.

Thanks to the 7.62 x 51mm Nato standard round, the FN FAL was a powerful weapon, capable of hitting targets up to 600m (1268ft) and in Africa it doubled as a big game weapon. The main drawback of the weapon was its long length, 1090mm (43in), and weight, 4.45kg (10lb). For this reason, most Nato armies started to phase the weapon out of service in the 1980s and replaced it with lighter 5.56mm 'bullpup' designs. It has remained popular on the second-hand market and still appears on Third World or Middle Eastern battlefields.

M16

In conflicts with a strong American involvement, the Colt M16 is bound to surface. The weapon is based on Eugene Stoner's original design, and since 1967 has been the official assault rifle of the US armed forces.

The first modern assault rifle to enter widespread service, the M16 utilizes 5.56 x 45mm ammunition, and compared to the FN FAL, it seems lightweight and

BELOW: A Royal Marine takes aim with an SLR rifle, the standard weapon of the British Army until the early 1980s. Accurate and reliable, it remains popular with mercenaries.

SDV DRAGUNOV

'plastic'. Weighing only 3kg (6.6lb), with a length of 991mm (39in), the weapon can fire 700 to 950 rounds a minute when fired on full automatic. Early versions were heavily criticized in Vietnam because of unreliability and flimsy construction. A new improved M16A1 version entered service to correct these shortcomings, and in 1982 the M16A2 was produced. This fires standard Nato 5.56mm ammunition, and has a three-round burst facility rather than the automatic capability.

If available, the M16A2 is the weapon of choice for mercenaries. It is far superior to any of the European bullpup 5.56mm designs, such as the British SA-80, and when combined with the M203 grenade launcher, it has awesome firepower. The mini M16, the Colt Commando, is highly popular with paramilitary forces and bodyguards because of its short length – 680mm (27in) with stock retracted, or 760mm (30in) with stock extended, and is America's answer to the Russian AKSU.

SUB-MACHINE GUNS

Heckler & Koch MP5

This German sub-machine gun is undoubtedly popular because of its accuracy, reliability, rate of fire and ammunition availability. H&K have a reputation for making classy weapons, and the MP5 is no exception. The use of a closed bolt operating system means it is one of the few sub-machine guns that does not spray out bullets in a random pattern at anything over 40m (131ft). With a well-zeroed weapon you can put bullets through the same hole at over 200m (656ft). It is also stoppage-free – an essential quality in a firefight – even with its firing rate of 800 rounds a minute. It uses universally available 9mm Parabellum ammunition, a big attraction for mercenaries on foreign assignments.

Britain's SAS used the MP5 during the 1981 Iranian Embassy hostage-rescue mission, but it had been popular with special forces units since the mid-1970s. Middle Eastern security forces, with their unlimited budgets, are particularly keen on it and its derivatives. The shortened 'Kurz', or K version, is the main rival to the AKSU-74 and Colt Commando for covert operators, being compact enough to be hidden in clothing.

Type: M16A2 assault rifle	**Rate of fire**: 700-950
Calibre: 5.56mm	rounds per minute (cyclic)
Weight:: 3.8kg (8.5lb)	**Feed**: 20- or 30-round
Length: 1m (39.37in)	detachable box magazine
Effective range: 800m	**Muzzle velocity**: 991m
(2625ft)	(3250ft) per second.

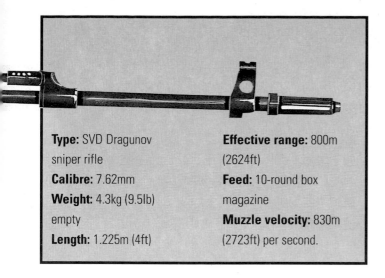

Type: SVD Dragunov sniper rifle	**Effective range:** 800m (2624ft)
Calibre: 7.62mm	**Feed:** 10-round box magazine
Weight: 4.3kg (9.5lb) empty	**Muzzle velocity:** 830m (2723ft) per second.
Length: 1.225m (4ft)	

Uzi

This Israeli-made weapon first appeared on the international arms market in large numbers during the early 1960s. Thanks to links between Congo's ruler Colonel Mobutu and the Jewish state, which trained his elite paratrooper regiments, it fell into the hands of mercenaries in the Congo.

Since then it has been popular with customers looking for short-range firepower. It is only 640mm (25in) long with the stock extended, so it can be easily concealed while still boasting an impressive 600-rounds-a-minute rate of fire. When fitted with a 40-round magazine, it is particularly useful for close-quarter battle, and the use of 9mm Parabellum ammunition makes resupply easy. Uzis have been made in Belgium, Germany and Croatia, as well as Israel, so it is easily available from black market sources at very reasonable prices.

SNIPER RIFLES

SDV Dragunov

The Soviet Army's standard sniper rifle since the mid-1960s has a distinctive shape and has become familiar worldwide. Exported to almost every war zone, this is the sniper rifle mercenaries are likely to encounter if they work in Eastern Europe or Third World war zones.

As the weapon is basically a sniper version of the AK, with a similar action, it is 'soldier proof' and very easy to use. Even the most illiterate peasant soldier can pick one up and start bumping off targets at up to 1000m (3280ft).

RIGHT: The General Purpose Machine Gun (GPMG), a medium machine gun designated L7 in British army service. It is extremely sturdy, and noted for its accuracy.

The Dragunov uses the powerful 7.62mm x 54 rimmed cartridge rather than standard AK ammunition.

It is only 1kg (2lb) heavier than the standard AK-47, at some 4.3kg (8.7lb), and 1225mm long (4ft). It is particularly useful to infantrymen without vehicles to move their heavy kit. With its PSO-1x4 scope, the Dragunov is credited with achieving single-shot kills at 800–1000m (2438–3280ft). The weapon was used by Soviet troops in Afghanistan and was also popular with snipers in the former Yugoslavia.

Zastava M76

This is the Yugoslav-made clone of the Dragunov, distinguished by its solid wooden shoulder butt. It is a very popular weapon with mercenaries in the former Yugoslavia because of its ease of operation and reliability. Like the Dragunov, it is based on the AK action, but the M76 is modelled on the Yugoslav-upgraded M70 assault rifle. The Yugoslav state armaments industry had a reputation for producing high-quality designs and high-standard weapons – the M76 is no exception. It had considerable flexibility built into it, with a universal sight

ABOVE: The Barrett .50 Model 82A1, a truly lethal weapon. A superb sniper's rifle, it is used by troops around the world and is highly regarded in mercenary circles.

mount enabling either optical or infra-red night sights to be fitted. Most versions found in use in former Yugoslavia are chambered to fire 7.92mm x 57 Mauser ammunition which is also used by the M53 General Purpose Machine Gun, so ammunition re-supply is very easy. Export versions have been chambered for 7.62mm x 51 Nato and 7.62mm x 54R Soviet rounds.

Barrett M82A1

This is a 'monster' sniper rifle weighing in at some 13.4kg (29.5lb). Thanks to its 12.7mm (.50 calibre) cartridge the Barrett will cut through even the thickest body armour at over 1000m (3280ft). It will also cause serious damage to lightly armoured vehicles, trucks, cars and helicopters.

Any mercenary wanting to kill from long distances will jump at the chance to use this weapon; it transforms a lightly armed outfit into a team of heavy hitters. In the

Gulf War it is credited with a kill at 1800m (5905ft). A number have been used by the Irish Republican Army (IRA) terrorists against British troops operating in Northern Ireland, and easily pierced the ceramic plates of British body armour from very long distances, inflicting fatal injuries.

The weapon is fitted with a telescopic sight and uses 11-round magazines. Unlike many other sniper rifles which retain bolt actions, it is a semi-automatic weapon. To minimise the recoil, a novel muzzle brake is fitted to divert much of the propellant gas sideways.

It is a far from small weapon, at 1.5m (5ft) long, and is impossible for men of average build to fire without the support of the bipod or window ledge for support.

MACHINE GUNS

FN MAG

Like the FN FAL rifle, this Belgian-designed weapon was widely exported during the 1950s and 1960s and was adopted by most Western-orientated armies as their standard section or platoon GPMG.

It was used extensively in the Congo, Rhodesia and Angola by mercenaries who were familiar with its impressive capabilities. With a cyclic rate of fire of between 750–1000 rounds a minute, it could lay down impressive firepower out to 1800m (5905ft). Being a belt-fed weapon, the FN MAG was designed to repel attacks on defensive positions. Many mercenaries in the Congo owed their lives to well-placed FN MAGs destroying rebel attacks.

Weighing 10.9kg (22lb), it is easily manportable during infantry assaults. Ammunition re-supply was always a problem, so Congo mercenaries tended to vehicle-mount the guns to keep them within easy reach of fresh belts of ammunition. It is still in service with many armies around the world.

ABOVE: The Browning High Power, one of the most popular handguns ever. Accurate up to 50m (164ft), it uses the widely-available 9mm ammunition.

BELOW: The .50-cal Browning M2 heavy machine gun. At 40kg (88lb), it is not exactly portable, and is more usually seen mounted on jeeps, or used for static defence.

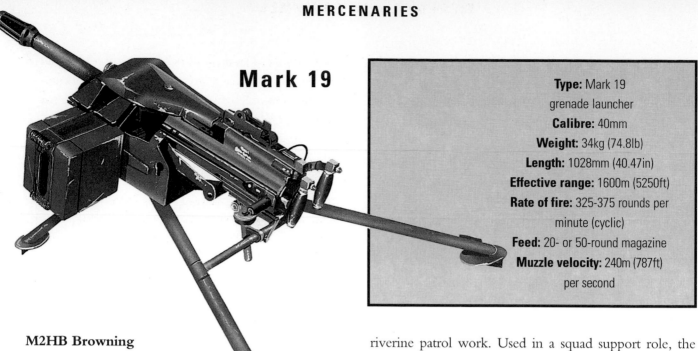

Mark 19

Type: Mark 19
grenade launcher
Calibre: 40mm
Weight: 34kg (74.8lb)
Length: 1028mm (40.47in)
Effective range: 1600m (5250ft)
Rate of fire: 325-375 rounds per
minute (cyclic)
Feed: 20- or 50-round magazine
Muzzle velocity: 240m (787ft)
per second

M2HB Browning

Ever since it entered service some 70 years ago, the 'Big Fifty' has dominated firefights around the world. Widely available, it has been used in many mercenary operations.

With a 2000m (6250ft) range and a .50-cal round, the M2HB has phenomenal stopping power. It can blast through light armour and is deadly against troops in the open, trucks, and low-flying aircraft. Weighing 40kg (81lb), without ammunition, the weapon is not really manportable and is most often used in the vehicle-mounted or static defensive role.

SUPPORT WEAPONS

Mark 19 grenade launcher

The Mark 19 grenade launcher was developed by the US Naval Ordnance Station during the Vietnam War in order to provide the US Navy with a suitable weapon for

riverine patrol work. Used in a squad support role, the Mark 19 can deliver a devastating barrage of 40mm grenades and has found favour with mercenary forces operating in Bosnia, Central America and Croatia. The weapon can fire a variety of rounds, including high explosive, smoke, armour-piercing, fragmentation, CS gas and illuminating types.

M72 Light Anti-tank Weapon

Manufactured in vast quantities for US forces heading for Vietnam, the LAW was widely available on the black market in the 1960s and 1970s. Weighing a mere 2.37kg (4.8lb), it was easily carried into battle by even the most heavily loaded infantrymen. Mercenaries loved the LAW

RPG-7

Type: RPG-7 anti-tank
rocket launcher
Calibre: 40mm (1.57in) for the launcher tube
Weight: 7kg (15.43lb)
Length: 0.99m (3ft 3in)
Rocket weight: 2.25kg (4.96lb) for the anti-tank type
Effective range: 500m (1640ft)
Armour penetration: 400mm (15.75in) at any range

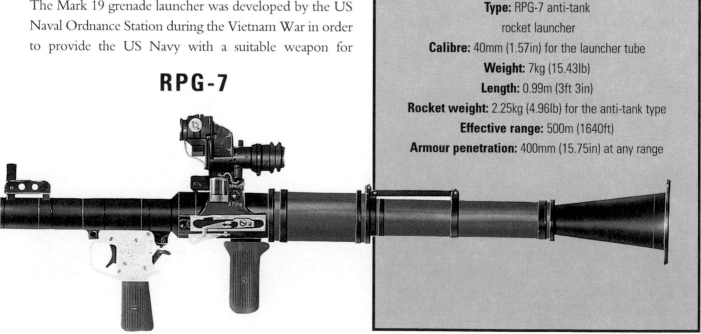

because it provided effective tank-killing power and could easily be used with the minimum of training. All you had to do was extend the weapon out of its plastic carrying tube and point it at the target. After use the empty tube was just thrown away.

It was effective at ranges up to 300m (984ft) against most tanks in use during the 1960s and 1970s. With the introduction of reactive and Chobham armour in the early 1980s, though, the weapon became obsolete. Mercenaries continue to use the LAW because of its important secondary role as a man-portable bunker buster.

RPG-7

Produced by the millions in Russian, Chinese, Yugoslavian and other nations' factories, this is the guerrilla's favourite weapon after his AK-47, and is the

rocket-propelled grenade launcher that the mercenary is most likely to encounter in Third World war zones.

Robust and easy to use, the main launcher unit is rested on the shoulder and the grenade is loaded in the front. A basic optic sight is fitted, but the weapon can be fired without using an iron sight. Weighing only 10kg (20lb) for one rocket and launcher, the RPG-7 is easily man-portable and will be found in the first wave of any infantry assault. It can hit targets up to 300 m (981ft). Modern reactive and Chobbam armour will defeat the older generation of RPG warheads, although newer ones are available in some war zones.

M79/M203 grenade launchers

The US-designed M79 was first used in the Vietnam War to provide infantry squads with direct stand-off firepower.

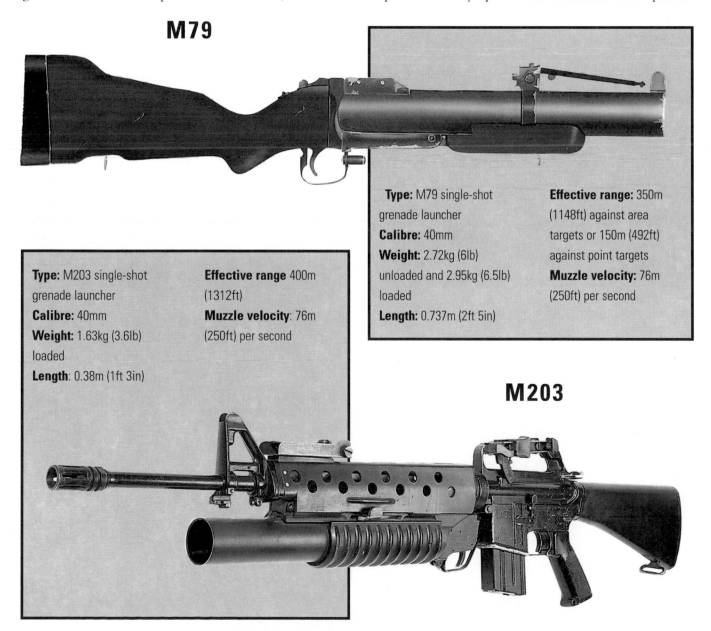

M79

Type: M79 single-shot grenade launcher
Calibre: 40mm
Weight: 2.72kg (6lb) unloaded and 2.95kg (6.5lb) loaded
Length: 0.737m (2ft 5in)

Effective range: 350m (1148ft) against area targets or 150m (492ft) against point targets
Muzzle velocity: 76m (250ft) per second

Type: M203 single-shot grenade launcher
Calibre: 40mm
Weight: 1.63kg (3.6lb) loaded
Length: 0.38m (1ft 3in)

Effective range 400m (1312ft)
Muzzle velocity: 76m (250ft) per second

M203

It was capable of firing high-explosive, smoke, CS gas and anti-personnel fléchette rounds up to 150m (492ft). To improve the utility of the weapon, the US Army developed the M203, which could be fitted to an M16 assault rifle. Mercenaries love the M16/M203 combination because it produces an easily carried, multi-role weapon system.

PERSONAL PROTECTION WEAPONS

9mm Browning

The good old Browning High Power has long been the mercenary's favourite personal protection weapon. Made by the millions since World War II, it is cheap, and spares are readily available. It uses the universally available 9mm Parabellum ammunition. At ranges under 50m (164ft) it is accurate and will stop a man in his tracks.

Makarov

Widely available in eastern Europe, the pistol of the former Red Army has been adopted by mercenaries, bodyguards and mafia hitmen all over the former Soviet Union. In terms of quality and reliability, it is not

BELOW: A BMP, an infantry fighting vehicle which is in service in the armies of former Warsaw Pact countries and throughout Africa. BMPs have often been pressed into mercenary service.

comparable to Western pistols, such as the Browning or SIG, but the widespread availability of its 9mm x 18 ammunition makes it a must for mercenaries operating in eastern Europe.

DAGGERS

When it comes to life or death hand-to-hand combat, mercenaries swear by the traditional World II Two-era Commando dagger. With a blade designed to penetrate the neck and chest, it is still useful. FN FAL and AK-47 bayonets are also much in demand as fighting blades.

HAND GRENADES

Standard fragmentation grenades are essential items for mercenaries. They provide close-range firepower for house and trench clearing. Smoke grenades are also useful; they are vital for marking helicopter landing zones and creating smoke screens to cover movement from enemy observation.

MOBILITY

Mil Mi-8 'Hip'

Now the most widely exported transport helicopter to Third World nations, the Mi-8 is a robust if basic design that can be fitted with guns, rocket pods and anti-tank

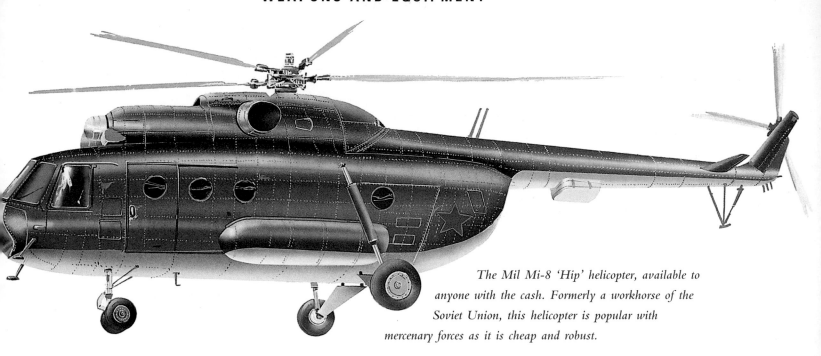

The Mil Mi-8 'Hip' helicopter, available to anyone with the cash. Formerly a workhorse of the Soviet Union, this helicopter is popular with mercenary forces as it is cheap and robust.

missiles. South Africa's Executive Outcomes regularly uses them because they are cheap to buy, and ex-Soviet pilots are willing to do anything, anywhere for money.

Bell UH-1 'Huey'

Made famous in Vietnam, the Huey has been sold to over 60 countries. Western-backed mercenary operations in the 1960s and 1970s almost always featured the Huey if helicopter support was necessary.

Mil Mi-24 'Hind'

Like its small brother the Mi-8, the Mi-24 is unofficially exported from Russia to anyone who will pay cash. Mercenary pilots have flown the Hind in the former Yugoslavia, Angola and Sierra Leone. As well as boasting twin 23mm cannon, rocket pods, bombs or anti-tank missiles, the Mi-24 can carry an infantry squad in its rear cargo cabin. Croatian Mi-24s were used to drop off teams behind enemy lines during the 1995 Operation Storm offensive that routed Serb forces in the Krajina region.

BELOW: A mobile recce. Land Rover vehicles have served mercenary forces well for nearly four decades. They are reliable, robust and can mount a variety of weapons.